100 THINGS TO DO IN PALM SPRINGS BEFORE YOU DIE

Tahquitz Falls
Photo Credit: Tom Brewster Photography

100 THINGS TO DO IN PALM SPRINGS BEFORE YOU DIE

LYDIA KREMER

Reedy Press
PO Box 5131
St. Louis, MO 63139, USA
reedypress.com

Library of Congress Control Number: 2016940396

ISBN: 9781681060514

Design by Jill Halpin

Cover Image: Tom Brewster Photography

Printed in the United States of America
16 17 18 19 20   5 4 3 2 1

Please note that websites, phone numbers, addresses, and company names are subject to change or cancellation. We did our best to relay the most accurate information available, but due to circumstances beyond our control, please do not hold us liable for misinformation. When exploring new destinations, please do your homework before you go.

DEDICATION

To my hero, Alex
and to
the memory of my mother, Carmen,
who loved Palm Springs

CONTENTS

Music and Entertainment

Sports and Recreation

Culture and History

Shopping and Fashion

PREFACE

You're about to discover 100 reasons why Palm Springs is a world-renowned, glamorous, and fun destination. But this is just the tip of the palm tree; there are way more than 100 reasons. I only wish the title was "1000 Things to Do…" because there are so many more wonderful places and things that I could not include.

Palm Springs is approximately 100 miles east of Los Angeles in the southern California desert. Ringed by breathtaking mountain vistas, the region is notable for its extraordinarily diverse and picturesque landscape.

Although the City of Palm Springs has the international brand recognition, it is but only one of nine distinct cities, each with its own cultural identity, that make up the Coachella Valley, an area approximately 35 miles in length. The nine cities, from west to east, are: Palm Springs, Desert Hot Springs (slightly north), Cathedral City, Rancho Mirage, Palm Desert, Indian Wells, La Quinta, Indio, and Coachella. However, because of Palm Springs's international fame, people generally refer to the Coachella Valley or Greater Palm Springs as "Palm Springs."

Note that many of the high profile annual events throughout the desert communities take place during "season" which is typically from about October through May. While summer is a slower pace, there are still plenty of activities to enjoy.

• •

As a resident of Palm Springs for nearly a quarter of a century, I've been an unabashed cheerleader for our unparalleled slice of paradise. I often tell visitors discovering the area's abundant charms for the first time, "you will think you died and went to heaven." It's a prediction borne out by the large numbers of visitors who are compelled to orchestrate their relocation and become residents of this sublime desert oasis.

So when Reedy Press asked me to write *100 Things to Do in Palm Springs Before You Die*, I was pleased to have the opportunity to illustrate my point.

The stark desert landscape as it merges with and abuts the soaring Santa Rosa and San Jacinto Mountains National Monument, with 10,000-foot peaks, is an intoxicating postcard image that will stay with you.

Whether you're a first-time visitor, a returning visitor, a new resident, or a long-time resident, I hope you'll find this guide a useful checklist of 100 ways to indulge yourself. Welcome to heaven!

—Lydia Kremer

ACKNOWLEDGMENTS

To all of those who inhabit the center of my circle—my beloved family, treasured friends, trusted colleagues, and adventurous fellow travelers—you know who you are. I thank you for your love, support, inspiration, and humor. Thank you too for joining me on life's exhilarating journey.

Special thanks to Tom Brewster, staff at *Palm Springs Life*, and the Greater CVB, for the dazzling photographs; Frank Jones for his friendship and professional collaboration over the years; Mary Jo Ginther and the Palm Springs Bureau of Tourism; and countless others for their enthusiastic support of this book.

Photo Credit: Point7West

Palm Desert Food & Wine Festival
Photo Credit: Michael Mathews

FOOD AND DRINK

FOOD
FOR THOUGHT

Discriminating palates won't have to look too far to get their foodie fix in Palm Springs. The desert communities boast a sophisticated culinary scene and host a variety of annual events devoted to elevating dining and imbibing to an art.

The major such event is the annual Palm Desert Food & Wine Festival, which takes place each March/April as part of the Palm Springs Life Festival—a month of music, fashion, food, and fun that culminates in the three-day Palm Desert Food & Wine culinary extravaganza. Celebrating its seventh annual event in 2017, it features more than 40 restaurants and numerous renowned chefs from around the country. The event kicks off with a prestigious James Beard Luncheon featuring celebrated chefs who prepare an unforgettable four-course lunch.

Palm Desert Food & Wine Festival
888-596-1027
palmdesertfoodandwine.com

FOOD
CELEBRATIONS

Greater Palm Springs hosts numerous other culinary-centric events throughout the year. The Greek Festival (February) is sponsored by the St. George Greek Orthodox Church of Palm Desert. This popular annual event marked its twentieth anniversary in 2016 and will continue the tradition celebrating all things Greek—authentic Greek food, live bouzouki music, and Greek dancing—held over two days in February (check website for dates). The Rhythm, Wine & Brews Experience (March) is an outdoor beer and wine fest featuring samples of craft beers and wine with more than 40 breweries and 30 wineries from around the state. Food trucks and booths provide the perfect pairings. The event also features continuous live music to add to the fun.

Greek Festival
St. George Greek Orthodox Church, 74109 Larrea, Palm Desert
760-568-9901
pdgreekfest.org

Rhythm, Wine & Brews Experience
Empire Polo Club, 81800 Avenue 51, Indio
760-342-2762
rwbexp.com

WHAT'S COOKIN'?

Enjoy a hands-on culinary experience with a cooking demonstration—a fun opportunity to enjoy wonderful cuisine in a whole new way. At Copley's, chef/owner Andrew Copley invites you to join him for a Happy Hour Cooking Class in his eponymous restaurant's courtyard gardens. Guests enjoy a glass of wine and hors d'oeuvres while observing an entertaining and instructive demonstration by Chef Copley. Guests who choose to stay for dinner will receive 20 percent off their food bill. Le Vallauris, the premier French restaurant in Palm Springs, has been a fine dining destination in the desert for 40 years. From November to May, Le Vallauris offers monthly cooking demonstrations by Executive Chef Jean Paul Lair and Pastry Chef Laurent Dellac. Enjoy a fabulous three-course meal following the demonstration and take home a booklet of the recipes.

Copley's
621 N. Palm Canyon Drive, Palm Springs
760-327-9555
copleyspalmsprings.com

Le Vallauris
385 W. Tahquitz Canyon Way, Palm Springs
760-325-5059
levallauris.com

HOT
TAMALES

The Indio International Tamale Festival (December) is a two-day event celebrating the rich cultural heritage of the humble tamale, which varies wildly within different cultures, and even within families, but is always a delectable treat. You can sample dozens of various tamales, from sweet to savory and from vegetarian to gluten free. The festival, held in the heart of Old Town Indio, takes place annually the first weekend in December. The Indio International Tamale Festival, which began in 1992, has received numerous accolades, most notably the Food Network's Top 10 list of "All-American Food Festivals." It has also been included in the Guinness Book of World Records for the world's largest tamale (one foot wide and 40 feet long) and the largest tamale festival based on attendance (120,000).

Indio International Tamale Festival
760-832-8620 Ext. 43
tamalefestival.net

CAMELS
AND CARNIVAL

At the 10-day Riverside County Fair and National Date Festival (February), you'll find a variety of tasty treats made with dates. The festival, an annual tradition since 1946, features a festive atmosphere and family fun, with nightly musical performances by notable artists. It also has a lively carnival atmosphere with camel rides, as well as 7,000 exhibits and booths offering crafts, food, and beverages. One of the highlights of the event is the crowning of Queen Scheherazade, a nod to the Middle Eastern origin of the date. You can sample a surprising variety of dishes made with the biblical fruit—candy, baked goods, jam, and more. Be sure to try a scrumptious date shake, a local specialty.

Riverside County Fair and National Date Festival
Riverside County Fairgrounds, 82503 Highway 111, Indio
800-811-3247
datefest.org

FUN FACT

While not native to the United States, dates were first introduced to the Coachella Valley at the turn of the last century as an effort by the U.S. Department of Agriculture to find crops from around the world that could be grown in the United States. Seedlings were brought to the Coachella Valley from the Middle East, and, due to the region's high temperatures and low humidity, dates have flourished. Date palms are iconic fixtures in the eastern portion of the Coachella Valley and a major boon to the economy of the region. Today, dates are an important (and delicious) agricultural industry in the Coachella Valley.

6

HOP
TO IT

The craft beer movement in Greater Palm Springs is well established and has several local breweries you'll want to visit for a taste and a tour. Babe's B-B-Que & Brewhouse has been brewing award-winning tasty hops since the early 2000s and has been a trendsetter in the desert. The legacy of the late founder, Don Callender, who founded the Marie Callender's restaurant chain, is savored in every sip. Coachella Valley Brewing Co. uses a state-of-the-art, 17-barrel brewhouse—a HEBS, or high-efficiency brewing system—one of only five such systems in the world. This high-tech process enables the brewery to produce a variety of stellar award-winning brews from locally sourced ingredients. La Quinta Brewing Co. has two tap rooms and produces several brews that have also won top honors statewide.

Babe's B-B-Que & Brewhouse
71800 Highway 111, Rancho Mirage
760-346-8738
babesbbqandbrewhouse.com

Coachella Valley Brewing Co.
30640 Gunther Street, Thousand Palms
760-343-5973
cvbco.com

La Quinta Brewing Co.
Brewery Taproom, 77917 Wildcat Drive, Palm Desert
760-200-2597

Old Town Taproom,
78065 Main Street #100, La Quinta
760 972-4251
laquintabrewing.com

EAT, DRINK, AND BE MERRY

Another culinary highlight is Palm Springs Desert Resorts Restaurant Week (June). You'll be singing the praises of the fabulous dining scene here, and if you time your visit right, you'll be able to eat your way through the desert cities for a song. Each year in June, Restaurant Week takes place throughout all the desert cities when local favorite restaurants offer a prix fixe lunch and dinner for bargain prices you that won't want to pass up. You'll be able to choose from 200 eateries—bistros, cafés, diners, and fine dining establishments. Restaurant Week also partners with many of the local hotels, which offer great rates and packages.

Palm Springs Desert Resorts Restaurant Week
760-322-8008
palmspringsrestaurantweek.com

8

IT'S 5:00 SOMEWHERE

The cocktail hour in Greater Palm Springs is a highlight of the day, a part of the lifestyle often enjoyed poolside. Watching the sun slip behind the mountains and seeing the light change to mauve and purple is a thrilling sight, made even more special with a cocktail in hand. Many Palm Springs establishments cater to this ritual in a big way with a range of specialty handcrafted cocktails on their lounge menu. Whether your style is a friendly neighborhood pub, a stylish modern bar, or a classic throwback watering hole, you'll find the perfect place for cocktails to fit your mood. There are several notable possibilities you should put on your list, and if your sunset happy hour runs long into the dinner hour, so much the better.

9

CHEERS
TO YOU!

Speaking of cocktails, try any of these suggested spots for a memorable cocktail hour experience with postcard views. Tommy Bahama's Restaurant, located on the upper floor of the Gardens on El Paseo shops, offers a large outdoor patio with sweeping views of the mountains. The Purple Palm Restaurant, located at the Colony Palms Hotel, offers memorable poolside signature cocktails and stunning views of the mountains—a winning combo. The Escena Lounge & Grill Restaurant, located at Escena Golf Club, has expansive views across the picturesque golf fairways that give way to gorgeous unobstructed mountain views. And if the name Elixir elicits visions of tempting libations, head over to The V Hotel, one of Palm Springs's new glam outposts. Elixir, their poolside tapas bar, serves up unforgettable craft cocktails and poolside DJ parties.

Tommy Bahama's Restaurant
73595 El Paseo, Palm Desert, 760-836-0188
http://tommybahama.com/restaurants/palm-desert

Purple Palm Restaurant at Colony Palms
572 N. Indian Canyon Drive, Palm Springs, 760-969-1818
colonypalmshotel/dining

Escena Lounge & Grill
1100 Clubhouse View, Palm Springs, 760-992-0002
escenagolf.com/dine

Elixir at The V Hotel
333 E. Palm Canyon Drive, Palm Springs, 877-544-4446,
vpalmsprings.com

INSIDER'S TIP

If you are planning to imbibe a few cocktails, take advantage of the City of Palm Springs's complimentary shuttle service called The Buzz. The colorful Buzz trolley makes a loop from one end of town to the other, with several stops. The free Buzz program has four trolleys that run every 15 minutes Thursday through Sunday from 11 a.m. until 1 a.m.

Search the route at buzzps.com.

DINING
ALFRESCO

With 360 days of sunshine, dining alfresco while happily ensconced on an outdoor patio is *de rigueur* in Palm Springs. Accordingly, numerous restaurants in the desert communities have lush outdoor patios, most of which offer heaters in winter and cooling misters in summer to keep guests comfortable year-round. Besides enjoying a meal outdoors, some restaurants in downtown Palm Springs offer great opportunities for our favorite sport: people-watching. In each of the Greater Palm Springs cities, there are countless possibilities for grabbing a casual meal or having a fine dining experience while enjoying the desert sunshine or evening air. The following are just a few eateries that have outdoor patios, great menus, and a friendly, welcoming atmosphere.

Eight4Nine Restaurant & Lounge
849 N. Palm Canyon Drive,
Palm Springs
760-325-8490
eight4nine.com

Pomme Frite
256 S. Palm Canyon Drive,
Palm Springs
760-778-3727
pommefrite.com

Mitch's on El Paseo
73951 El Paseo,
Palm Desert
760-779-9200
mitchsonelpaseo.com

Spencer's
701 W. Baristo Road,
Palm Springs
760-327-3446
spencersrestaurant.com

INSIDER'S TIP

Here's a tip for navigating your way through the Coachella Valley. California State Highway 111 runs through eight of the nine cities that comprise Greater Palm Springs. While searching for a particular address on Highway 111, be sure you identify in which city the business is located. Also note that in Palm Springs the main thoroughfare is called Palm Canyon Drive, with sections of the street referred to as North Palm Canyon Drive, East Palm Canyon Drive, or South Palm Canyon Drive. If you are trying to locate a business on Palm Canyon Drive, make note whether the address is North, South, or East Palm Canyon Drive, and you'll find your destination more easily.

11

A CUP
OF JOE

The nation's trend for coffee snobbery certainly hasn't passed Greater Palm Springs by. Whether you're looking for a java jolt as a quick pick-me-up in the afternoon or wanting a leisurely morning cuppa with your pals to catch up, there's a perfect spot for you just minutes away from your location in the desert. One of the most popular coffee hangouts is Koffi, with two locations in Palm Springs and a third one in Rancho Mirage. Koffi sources, roasts, and brews its own beans to suit even the most discriminating coffee drinkers. In the heart of downtown Palm Springs, Joey Palm Springs provides a friendly neighborhood atmosphere where you can watch the world go by in the pleasant outdoor patio while sipping San Francisco's Equator Coffee and Teas with freshly made breakfast, lunch, or dinner specialties.

Koffi
515 N. Palm Canyon Drive, Palm Springs
760-416-2244
1700 S. El Camino Real, Palm Springs
760-322-7776
71380 Highway 111, Rancho Mirage
760-340-2444
koffi.com

Joey Palm Springs
245 S. Palm Canyon Drive, Palm Springs
760-320-8370
joeyps.com

12

THE MOST IMPORTANT MEAL OF THE DAY

Just like Mom told you, don't skip breakfast. Breakfast is a celebration to begin your day and jump-start your engine. Whether you want a "grab 'n go" or a comforting full breakfast Mom would be proud of, there are several standout breakfast restaurants around the desert cities. Wilma and Frieda's Café is a great spot to fortify yourself before a day of shopping at the Gardens on El Paseo. Elmer's has been a Palm Springs locals' favorite since 1960. A more recent locals' fave is Cheeky's, which offers a changing, creative menu—a bacon flight is a house specialty. La Quinta Baking Company features a bakery and casual French fare. Don and Sweet Sue's Café has been a locals' favorite go-to for comfort food in Cathedral City.

Wilma and Frieda's Café
73575 El Paseo, Palm Desert
760-773-2807
wilmafrieda.com

Elmer's
1030 E. Palm Canyon Drive, Palm Springs
760-327-8419
eatatelmers.com

Cheeky's
622 N. Palm Canyon Drive, Palm Springs
760-327-7595
cheekysps.com

La Quinta Baking Company
78395 Highway 111, La Quinta
760-777-1699
laquintabaking.com

Don and Sweet Sue's Café
68955 Ramon Road #1, Cathedral City
760-770-2760
donandsweetsues.com

13

DINING
IN THE CLOUDS

One of Palm Springs's most popular attractions is the Palm Springs Aerial Tramway (see more on page 57 in Sports and Recreation). The 10-minute ride takes you up the face of Mount San Jacinto to an elevation of 8,500 feet and is a wonder in itself. The rotating cars transport you two and a half miles from the desert floor up to the Mountain Station, where you'll find yourself surrounded by pine forests. You can purchase a ticket for the tram ride only or opt for a Ride 'n Dine ticket that includes lunch or dinner. Cap off your thrill ride with a drink and a meal at one of the dining options. Peaks Restaurant offers fine dining with sensational views. The Pines Café is a more casual restaurant but with equally splendid views. Before or after your meal, sip and savor a drink at the Lookout Lounge.

Peaks Restaurant and the Pines Cafe
Palm Springs Aerial Tramway, 1 Tramway Road,
Palm Springs
760-325-1391
pstramway.com

Palm Springs Aerial Tramway
Photo Credit:
Chris Miller

14

MEMORABLE MEALS—
FINE DINING

Fine dining in the desert has been elevated to the status of a VIP special event. You'll find an array of exceptional fine dining establishments here with sophisticated cuisine to satisfy any foodie. Here are just a few standouts, both large and small, and all equally wonderful. Johannes has a menu of excellent European and Austrian food inspired by chef/owner Johannes Bacher's roots. Lavender Bistro, a family-owned restaurant, has its roots in exceptional French cuisine. The Steakhouse doubles your pleasure with two locations. The elegant dining rooms offer outstanding steaks as well as veal, lamb, and seafood. Wally's Desert Turtle has been a fine dining institution in the desert since 1978. Dining at Le Vallauris, located off the beaten path, is a culinary celebration that won't disappoint.

Johannes
196 S. Indian Canyon Drive, Palm Springs
760-778-0017
johannesrestaurants.com

Lavender Bistro (dinner only)
78073 Calle Barcelona, La Quinta
760-564-5353
lavenderbistro.com

The Steakhouse
Agua Caliente Casino Resort Spa,
32250 Bob Hope Drive, Rancho Mirage
hotwatercasino.com

Spa Resort Casino
401 E. Amado Road, Palm Springs
sparesortcasino.com

888-999-1995 (for both)

Wally's Desert Turtle
71775 Highway 111, Rancho Mirage
760-568-9321
wallysdesertturtle.com

Le Vallauris
385 W. Tahquitz Canyon Way, Palm Springs
760-325-5059
levallauris.com

BEST
BUNS

Since hamburgers are an original Southern California tradition (McDonald's and In-N-Out started here), it's not surprising that Tyler's in Palm Springs has been touted as one of the top five burger joints in the state. The Zagat-rated eatery, located in the historic La Plaza in downtown Palm Springs, is in a league of its own for burgers and hot dogs. Tyler's offers straightforward and delicious burgers and sliders with a choice of sides, including its signature potato salad and coleslaw, which has been described as legendary. Pair your burger with Tyler's freshly made lemonade or indulge yourself with an old-fashioned milk shake. The place is only open for lunch and accepts strictly cash. Warren Buffett and Bill Gates have been known to drop in for burgers and a meeting of minds. The wait line at Tyler's speaks for itself but is well worth the wait. Be sure to check before you go. Tyler's is closed for a few weeks in the summer.

Tyler's Burgers
149 S. Indian Canyon Drive, Palm Springs
760-325-2990
tylersburgers.com

16

IT'S
A DATE

Date shakes are a delicious local tradition that was born out of the region's significant date production. Shields Date Garden is one of the original date producers, and its roadside stand that began in 1924 has morphed into a large operation that includes 17 acres of date gardens, a gift store featuring a large variety of dates to take home, a café with a sunny patio, and an old-fashioned fountain-type counter where you can order one of their signature date shakes. Shields also has a small theatre where you can watch *The Romance and Sex Life of the Date*, a free film that tells the history of the date, how the fruit is grown and produced, and fascinating facts you never knew.

Shields Date Garden
80225 Highway 111, Indio
760-347-0996
shieldsdategarden.com

TASTE
AND STROLL

What can be better than sampling tasty treats and walking it off—a guilt-free indulgence! Desert Tasty Tours offers just that. With their three-hour culinary crawls, you'll enjoy tasty samples at several restaurants and shops within a comfortable one-mile radius for an easy and casual stroll. Tours are conducted by a knowledgeable local guide who will share interesting cultural and historical factoids along the route. You can choose from two tours in different locations or try them both for a totally different but tasty experience. Each is followed by a great lunch. One tour is along the El Paseo Shopping District in Palm Desert and one is along Palm Canyon Drive in downtown Palm Springs. Tours are offered from October to June.

Desert Tasty Tours
800-979-3370
deserttastytours.com

18

SWEETS FOR
THE SWEET

What would a day be without a sweet indulgence? Sure, you'll find See's Candies in a couple of Coachella Valley locations, but give our locally produced handcrafted candies a try. Palm Springs Fudge & Chocolates was originally called Heiminger's when it opened in 1994 and featured fudge from Mackinac Island, Michigan. It is still family operated and prides itself on the highest-quality old-fashioned fudge, truffles, toffee, and chocolates. Brandini Toffee began as a fundraising effort for two high school pals and turned their award-winning almond toffee recipe into a nationally known product now found at retailers around the country, including 25 West Coast Nordstroms. Drop by the Rancho Mirage facility for a tour or swing by Palm Springs Toffee Shop for a free sample—you'll be hooked.

Brandini Toffee
42250 Bob Hope Drive,
Rancho Mirage
760-200-1598

Palm Springs Toffee Shop
132 S. Palm Canyon Drive,
Palm Springs
760-200-1598

Palm Springs Fudge & Chocolates
211 S. Palm Canyon Drive, Palm Springs
760-416-0075
palmspringsfudgeandchocolates.com

19

ETHNIC DINING:
ITALIAN

Maybe it's because Ol' Blue Eyes demanded excellent authentic Italian food while he lived in Palm Springs that the desert communities have such exceptional Italian cuisine. Many current restaurants would make Mr. Sinatra proud. Owned by two Castelli brothers, Castelli's Ristorante has been consistently voted a locals' favorite. Among their house specialties that garner raves are Chef Brian Altman's Fettuccini Alfredo. The owners of Il Giardino brought their excellent authentic Northern Italian cuisine directly to Palm Springs from Milan after relocating in 2015. Johnny Costa's menu features some of Frank Sinatra's favorite dishes that Mr. Costa was invited to personally prepare at Sinatra's home. Family-run Spaghetteria Pasta & Pizza features terrific food and is a friendly neighborhood eatery where "Mama" may bid you "hello" from the kitchen. La Spiga Ristorante's menu features everything made from scratch, with high-quality organic ingredients.

INSIDER'S TIP

Because Greater Palm Springs has been an international tourist destination for decades, we have no shortage of international cuisine options to choose from. Your palate can take a trip around the world with the range of restaurants specializing in a variety of ethnic and international cuisines.

Castelli's Ristorante
73098 Highway 111, Palm Desert
760-773-3365
castellis.cc

Il Giardino
333 S. Indian Canyon Drive, Palm Springs
760-322-0888
ilgiardinopalmsprings.com

Johnny Costa's
440 S. Palm Canyon Drive, Palm Springs
760-325-4556
johnnycostaspalmsprings.com

Spaghetteria Pasta & Pizza
611 S. Palm Canyon Drive, Palm Springs
760-322-7647

La Spiga Ristorante
72557 Highway 111, Palm Desert
760-340-9318
laspigapalmdesert.com

20

ETHNIC DINING:
MEXICAN

If you're hankering for tasty Mexican fare, each of the nine cities in Greater Palm Springs can claim some of the best Mexican food in Southern California. We've narrowed down the options with a disclaimer: these are not the only great places from which to choose. The El Mexicali Café, the oldest woman-owned Mexican eatery in the desert, serves authentic, tasty Mexican food at three locations. The next best thing to a taco food truck is El Jefe, which serves delectable street tacos at The Saguaro Hotel. The Las Casuelas chain has had a long history that started in 1958 in Palm Springs. Since then, the five children of founders Florencio and Maria Delgado have each opened a Casuelas restaurant in cities across Greater Palm Springs.

El Mexicali Café
82720 Indio Boulevard, Indio
760-347-1280
elmexicalicafe.com

El Jefe at Saguaro Hotel
1800 E. Palm Canyon Drive, Palm Springs
760-322-1900
jdvhotels.com/restaurants/the-saguaro-palmsprings/el-jefe

The Original Las Casuelas
368 N. Palm Canyon Drive, Palm Springs
760-325-3213
theoriginallascasuelas.com

Las Casuelas Terraza
222 S. Palm Canyon Drive, Palm Springs
760-325-2794
lascasuelas.com

Las Casuelas Nuevas
70050 Highway 111, Rancho Mirage
760-328-8844
lascasuelasnuevas.com

Las Casuelas Quinta
78480 Highway 111, La Quinta
760-777-7715
lascasuelasquinta.com

Casuelas Café
73703 Highway 111, Palm Desert
760-568-0011

21

ETHNIC DINING:
THAI/VIETNAMESE

Greater Palm Springs also has its share of restaurants specializing in wonderful Asian food. Pepper's Thai serves reliably delectable Thai specialties at reasonable prices. Thai Smile has two locations serving savory Thai dishes in a refined and relaxing ambiance. In Desert Hot Springs, Thai Palms Restaurant has been serving healthy, genuine Thai cuisine for 15 years. For Vietnamese cuisine, try Rooster And The Pig, whose menu features classic Vietnamese specialties with an American twist. This place has a lively atmosphere with a full bar and house cocktails. Or check out Viet-fusion Pho 533, which serves fresh, healthy, and savory Vietnamese pho, banh mi sandwiches, spring rolls, and more. The original owner named it Pho 533 for Land Transport Tanker 533, the vessel that carried her and her family from war-torn Vietnam to America in 1975.

Pepper's Thai Cuisine
396 N. Palm Canyon Drive, Palm Springs
760-322-1259
peppersthai.com

Thai Smile
100 S. Indian Canyon Drive, Palm Springs
760-320-5503
thaismilepalmsprings.com

73725 El Paseo, Palm Desert
760-341-6565
thaismilerm.com

Thai Palms Restaurant
12070 Palm Drive, Desert Hot Springs
760-288-3934
thaipalmdhs.com

The Rooster and The Pig
356 S. Indian Canyon Drive, Palm Springs
760-832-6691
roosterandthepig.com

Pho 533
1775 E. Palm Canyon Drive, Suite 625, Palm Springs
760-778-6595
pho533palmsprings.com

A DEEP
SUBJECT

The annual Deep Pit Barbeque at Los Compadres, a not-to-be-missed local tradition since 1941, reflects a bit of Palm Springs's equestrian history. Los Compadres is one of the oldest riding clubs in Palm Springs; its membership spans several generations of local families. The private equestrian club throws its doors open to the public once a year for this "Old West" event. Held the first weekend in November, the Los Compadres Annual Deep Pit Barbeque features beef that is slow-cooked for 24 hours in a 6-foot deep cement barbeque pit. The event, held outdoors at the Los Compadres clubhouse, is a fun and festive evening with music and frivolity. The western BBQ feast is served with ranch beans, coleslaw, and homemade cookies. Beer and wine are available for purchase, too.

Los Compadres Riding Club
1849 S. El Cielo, Palm Springs
760-322-2218

23

CONVIVIALITY
IN A GLASS

Wine enthusiasts should head to Desert Wines & Spirits for wine tastings held each Saturday from 4 to 5:30 p.m.; there's a $10 charge for the tasting, but $5 of that can be applied to any purchase. Hosted by owners Costa and Zola Nichols, these convivial wine tastings are fun gatherings of residents and visitors alike who share the love of wine. Even if you aren't too knowledgeable about wine, you are assured to leave a lot smarter. Each week, Costa, one of the foremost wine experts in the area, curates a special wine tasting that showcases a different wine, varietal, or country. The Tasting Room is open for individual or group tastings every day. Go Deli and Gourmet Market is also on-site and offers great sandwiches and the perfect items for pairing.

Desert Wines & Spirits & Go Deli Gourmet Market
611 S. Palm Canyon Drive, Suite 22, Palm Springs
760-327-7701
desertwinesandspirits.com

CASUAL
BUT TASTY

If you're looking for a casual environment but don't want to compromise on the quality of food, you're in luck. Greater Palm Springs has a multitude of great, unfussy eateries to fit your taste, mood, and budget. Many of these spots are popular local favorites. Wolfgang Puck's WP Kitchen + Bar in Palm Desert is the perfect intersection of culinary excellence and a relaxed chic atmosphere. Since 1976, John's Restaurant has been the perfect place to drop in for a hearty breakfast, a quick lunch, or a casual dinner. Place your order at the counter, grab a seat, and your order appears quickly. For a taste of American fare—biscuits, waffles, burgers, and milk shakes—try Keedy's Fountain Grill, a friendly spot with an old-fashioned counter.

WP Kitchen + Bar
73130 El Paseo, Suite 1, Palm Desert
760-568-2700
wolfgangpuck.com

John's Restaurant
900 N. Palm Canyon Drive,
Palm Springs
760-327-8522
johnsrestaurantpalmsprings.com

Keedy's Fountain Grill
73633 California Highway 111, Palm Desert
760-346-6492
keedysfountaingrill.com

DELI[CIOUS]
TAKE-OUT OR DINE-IN

Jake's has the best of both worlds—a deli case of tempting prepared choices to take home and a terrific menu featuring daily soups, great salads, and tasty entrees for dining in on their cheerful, friendly patio. Clementine Gourmet Marketplace & Café includes a deli, pasta bar, and patisserie. You can take out from the deli case featuring Spanish, French, and Italian selections, or dine in the friendly space of communal tables. Stop in at Clementine's boutique, which has beautiful imported gift items. For a hearty breakfast, lunch, or dinner, you can't go wrong at Sherman's Deli, a local institution. Sherman's didn't get the memo about portion control—their portions are enormous, perfect for sharing. Sherman's also offers kosher items on the menu, as well as a bakery case with to-die-for pastries, all made on the premises.

Jake's
664 N. Palm Canyon Drive,
Palm Springs
760-327-4400
jakespalmsprings.com

Clementine
72990 El Paseo, Palm Desert
760-834-8814
clementineshop.com

Sherman's Deli and Bakery
401 E. Tahquitz Canyon Way,
Palm Springs
760-325-1199

73161 Country Club Drive,
Palm Desert
760-568-1350
shermansdeli.com

The Show concert venue at the
Agua Caliente Resort Spa
Photo Credit:
Courtesy of the Agua Caliente
Casina Resort Spa

MUSIC AND ENTERTAINMENT

DANCING CHEEK
TO CHEEK

Drop in to the Casablanca Lounge at Melvyn's Restaurant any night of the week for free live music and dancing and you just might rub elbows with a celebrity. Located at the historic Ingleside Inn, Melvyn's has been a magnet for celebrities throughout its 40-plus-year history. The roster of luminaries who have been spotted there reads like a Hollywood Who's Who—Frank Sinatra, Liza Minnelli, Norah Jones, Virginia Madsen, John Travolta, Kirsten Dunst, and Cher are just a few. New Hollywood has also been drawn to the legendary hotspot for its authenticity—Melvyn's is one of the only remaining vestiges of Old Palm Springs where things have remained the same; in fact, you may think you are in a '70s disco time warp.

Casablanca Lounge at Melvyn's Restaurant
200 W. Ramon Road, Palm Springs
760-325-2323
inglesideinn.com/melvyns

RAT PACK
FAME

Known as one of the Rat Pack's Palm Springs hangouts, the Purple Room Supper Club is a stylish retro supper club that opened in 1960 and was a frequent watering hole for Frank, Dean, Sammy, and the rest of the Pack. It features live entertainment and a full dinner menu. Enjoy nightly happy hour, complimentary entertainment on Tuesdays, Wednesdays, Thursdays, and late night on Fridays, or make it date night for the Purple Room's Mainstage ticketed shows on most Friday, Saturday, and Sunday evenings. Reservations are required for reserved seating for the weekend Mainstage dinner shows, but you can snag a bar stool and belly up to the bar to enjoy the show.

Purple Room Supper Club
1900 E. Palm Canyon Drive, Palm Springs
760-322-4422
purpleroompalmsprings.com

FUN FACT

During its history, Palm Springs has been the glamorous playground for countless stars who escaped the glare of Hollywood, a tradition that still continues today. One of the early celebrities was Frank Sinatra, who first arrived in Palm Springs in the 1940s. In 1947, he built a home that became a magnet for many of his pals—Dean Martin, Sammy Davis Jr., Peter Lawford, and Joey Bishop—who collectively became known as the Rat Pack. Local tales about the fun-loving raconteurs's antics are legendary.

MUSIC'S
IN THE AIR

Palm Springs is renowned for inhabiting the intersection of fun, glamour, and sunshine. Those attributes offer the ideal backdrop for its dynamic music scene and major music festivals. Among the world's granddaddies of music festivals is the Coachella Valley Music and Arts Festival, held on two consecutive weekends each April at the Empire Polo Club in Indio. Since its inaugural event in 1999, Coachella has continued to grow exponentially and now draws more than 200,000 attendees from around the globe. While it's still dedicated to its alternative musical roots, Coachella features a variety of musical genres, including EDM, rock, hip-hop, and more. The event's mix of major international headlining acts and emerging new talent has made this the most successful music festival in the world. Accordingly, tickets sell out fast.

Coachella Valley Music and Arts Festival
81-800 Avenue 51, Indio
888-512-7469
coachella.com

29

MORE MUSIC
CELEBRATIONS

The Coachella Valley Music and Arts Festival might not be your cup of tea, but not to worry, no matter what your musical tastes, you'll be sure to find a music festival in the desert that will be just the thing. Goldenvoice, the force behind Coachella, also produces the Stagecoach Country Music Festival, a three-day country music fest that takes place a few weeks after Coachella in the same location at the Empire Polo Club in Indio. The Palm Springs Women's Jazz Festival (September) brings together legendary female jazz musicians as well as up-and-coming jazz talents for multiple days at the Annenberg Theater, and culminates with a Sunday brunch. The Joshua Tree Music Festival (May and October), billed as a "family friendly global music experience," throws in art, yoga, and organic foods to round out the four-day high desert music fest held twice a year.

Stagecoach Country Music Festival
81-800 Avenue 51, Indio
stagecoachfestival.com

Palm Springs Women's Jazz Festival
101 Museum Drive, Palm Springs
760-416-3545
pswomensjazzfestival.com

Joshua Tree Music Festival
joshuatreemusicfestival.com

30

A SLICE OF
PALM SPRINGS LIFE

A new addition to the diverse and sophisticated cultural scene in Greater Palm Springs is the Palm Springs Life Festival, which launched its inaugural event in March 2016. Reminiscent of the renowned 10-day Edinburgh Festival that has been a staple of Scotland's art and music scene since 1947, the Palm Springs Life Festival is destined to join the ranks of the world's most ambitious cultural celebrations. The four-week event has a broad focus on music, arts, fashion, and food, with a heavy emphasis on fun. It takes place in a variety of venues and includes performances by world-renowned artists. The festival presents Fashion Week El Paseo and concludes with Palm Desert Food & Wine. The Palm Springs Life Festival is produced by *Palm Springs Life* magazine.

Palm Springs Life Festival
palmspringslifefestival.com

INSIDER'S TIP

Palm Springs Life magazine has been the voice of the desert communities for more than 60 years. Pick up the latest copy during your visit to get up to speed on the current happenings in music, film, fashion, events, shopping, dining, design, real estate, and much more.

31

PERFORMING
ARTS SHOWCASE

The McCallum Theatre, named for a local pioneering family, was among the very earliest performing and cultural arts entities in Greater Palm Springs. Since its auspicious opening night in 1988—a star-studded affair attended by the likes of Bob Hope, President Gerald Ford, Lucille Ball, and Sarah Brightman—the McCallum Theatre has presented world-class music, dance, theater, comedy, and opera performances each season since. The elegant McCallum, with a capacity of 1,127, is a cultural gem in the desert and is a valued community and educational partner. The McCallum Institute is a philanthropic arm of the theatre whose mission is promoting the arts to local children and students. Among the notable headliners appearing at the McCallum have been Michael Feinstein, Placido Domingo, Shirley MacLaine, Kenny G, and many other legendary entertainers.

McCallum Theatre
73000 Fred Waring Drive, Palm Desert
760-340-2787
mccallumtheatre.com

AN OASIS
FOR PERFORMANCE

In addition to the McCallum Theatre, you will discover many more performing arts venues, both large and small, that offer a broad spectrum of music, theater, and more. Among the other venues: the Annenberg Theater, located in the lower level of the Palm Springs Art Museum, presents a variety of productions, including some of Broadway's best; Dezart Performs is a non-profit theatrical organization that produces high-quality theatre focusing on new and never-before-seen plays; the Palm Canyon Theatre, an intimate theater setting in a historic building, presents Broadway musicals and classical productions; and the Indio Performing Arts Center features music, comedy, and stage productions.

Annenberg Theater
101 Museum Drive, Palm Springs
760-325-4490
psmuseum.org/annenberg-theater

Dezart Performs
760-322-0179
dezartperforms.org

Palm Canyon Theatre
538 N. Palm Canyon Drive, Palm Springs
760-323-5123
palmcanyontheatre.org

Indio Performing Arts Center
45175 Fargo Street, Indio
760-775-5200
indioperformingartscenter.org

CONCERT SERIES
ON THE LAWN

Grab a picnic lunch and head to the Great Lawn at Sunnylands Center & Gardens for its annual Music in the Gardens concert series every Sunday afternoon throughout the month of March, but it's worth a visit any time of year. The Sunnylands Center & Gardens, a 200-acre site, is free and the public is invited to enjoy a stroll in the gardens before or after the concert. Bring a lawn chair and enjoy a different musical act on each consecutive Sunday in March from 11 a.m. to 1 p.m. The concert series features vocalists and musicians who perform a variety of musical genres including jazz, blues, classical, pop, and more. Large coolers and ice chests are not permitted, but the café offers non-alcoholic drinks as well as sandwiches and salads.

Sunnylands Center & Gardens
37977 Bob Hope Drive, Rancho Mirage
760-202-2222
sunnylands.org

SINGING UNDER
SUN AND SKY

Love Mozart, Verdi, and Puccini? As the saying goes, the best things in life are free, and such is the case with the annual Opera in the Park, which has become a beloved springtime tradition in Palm Springs since 1998. Produced by the Palm Springs Opera Guild of the Desert, the event has grown from an event for opera lovers to a much-anticipated annual event for families and people of all ages who may not be opera fans but love the outdoor performances by a talented cast of professional opera singers accompanied by a live orchestra. Attendees are invited to bring chairs, blankets, and picnics to enjoy a pleasant afternoon under the trees, listening to the voices of angels singing favorite opera arias. And, of course, it's free!

Opera in the Park at Sunrise Park
401 S. Pavilion Way, Palm Springs
palmspringsoperaguild.org

MUSIC ON
THE RESERVATION

One of the many unique aspects that makes Greater Palm Springs a culturally vibrant experience is that some of the areas either sit on or are adjacent to several tribal reservations. Each tribal reservation here boasts a world-class casino/resort that presents a variety of high-caliber entertainment. The Agua Caliente Band of Cahuilla Indians has two such venues—Spa Resort Casino in Palm Springs and The Show at Agua Caliente Spa Resort Casino in Rancho Mirage. The Cabazon Band of Mission Indians has Fantasy Springs Resort Casino in Indio, and Spotlight 29 Casino in Coachella is a business venture of the Twenty-Nine Palms Band of Mission Indians. Each of these venues presents major headliners in comedy, pop, rock 'n roll, big band, hip-hop, tribute performers, illusionists, and more. Check their websites for schedules and tickets.

Spa Resort Casino
401 E. Amado Road, Palm Springs
888-999-1995
sparesortcasino.com

Agua Caliente Casino Resort Spa
32250 Bob Hope Drive,
Rancho Mirage
888-999-1995
hotwatercasino.com

Spotlight 29
46200 Harrison Place, Coachella
800-585-3737
spotlight29.com

Fantasy Springs Resort Casino
84245 Indio Springs Parkway, Indio
800-827-2946
fantasyspringsresort.com

SPLISH-SPLASH

Leave it to a town like Palm Springs to come up with the wholly unique and fun concept of a progressive pool party. Splash House Pool & Music Festival is just that. Think . . . a very hip and sexy summer camp. Twice a year in the summer months, Splash House partners with several local hotels that host pool parties with DJs, poolside cocktails, and complimentary shuttle service for paid guests to hop from one venue to the next without worrying about driving. Splash House has presented major musical artists such as Moby, Cut Copy, Chromeo, Anna Lunoe, and Claude VonStroke. The poolside dance fest has grown in stature as a springboard for emerging musical talents, even drawing notice from *Billboard* magazine.

Splash House
splashhouse.com

INSIDER'S TIP

Splash House tends to draw millennials but is open to all ages who enjoy swaying and dancing to upbeat tunes while cooling their heels in a pool. Because it caters to the tech-savvy millennial crowd, all ticket transactions are done online. You can purchase single tickets or a package that gives you Splash House access and accommodations.

CELEBRATE
SINATRA'S LEGACY

Relive the musical magic of the world's best crooner. Frank Sinatra's phenomenal musical legacy is celebrated at the hugely popular Frank DiSalvo Show on Thursday, Friday, and Saturday nights at the Indian Wells Resort Hotel. DiSalvo is a talented singer in his own right and his renditions of the "Chairman of the Board's" repertoire will make you swoon. Just for fun, DiSalvo throws in a few tunes by Sinatra's Rat Pack pal Dean Martin and other sentimental audience favorites from the Great American Song Book. The Indian Wells Resort has live entertainment every night featuring a roster of seasoned professional singers and musicians offering a range of musical genres, from jazz to country to rock. Some nights even offer dance lessons. Check the schedule on the website; reservations are recommended.

Frank DiSalvo Show
Indian Wells Resort Hotel, 76661 Highway 111, Indian Wells
760-345-6466, ext. 7584
indianwellsresort.com

WORDS
AND MUSIC

A music concert in a library? Yup. The Rancho Mirage Library presents an International Classical Concert Series as well as many other musical performances throughout the year. Many of us grew up when libraries were quiet places that existed strictly to explore the world of books and information. No longer. To experience the dramatic evolution of how libraries have become vital community gathering places, head over to the Rancho Mirage Public Library which provides local residents and visitors alike with wonderful cultural programs. The range of engaging public events are broad and include film screenings, lectures, concerts, exhibits, family nights, children's story times, book discussions, and more. Some of the concerts have an admission fee, but many programs are free to the public.

Rancho Mirage Library
71100 Highway 111, Rancho Mirage
760-341-7323
ranchomiragelibrary.org

BNP Paribas Open at the
Indian Wells Tennis Garden
Photo Credit: Greater Palm Springs CVB

SPORTS AND RECREATION

TENNIS
ANYONE?

If it's March in Greater Palm Springs, you should head to the BNP Paribas Open at the Indian Wells Tennis Garden to catch all the top-tier tennis players in the world. The tournament, held each year in early March, is the first of nine ATP World Tour Masters series and is held in one of the world's best tennis stadiums. The Indian Wells Tennis Garden, owned by billionaire Larry Ellison, co-founder and CEO of Oracle Corporation, is the world's second-largest tennis venue. During the past couple of years, Ellison has invested a hefty sum to upgrade and add additional tennis stadiums and amenities to enhance the visitor experience tenfold. Situated on nearly 60 acres, the Indian Wells Tennis Garden features two state-of-the-art stadiums with 24,000 seats, plus dining, shopping, and entertainment, all in a stunning setting.

Indian Wells Tennis Garden
78200 Miles Avenue, Indian Wells
760-200-8400
bnpparibasopen.com

A THRILL
RIDE

The Palm Springs Aerial Tramway is a unique year-round thrill ride. The Aerial Tramway, opened in 1963, has the world's largest rotating tramcars. The cars take visitors on a 2.5-mile ride up the side of the mountain, from the desert floor to a pine forest in 10 minutes, during which riders will experience a temperature difference of 30 to 40 degrees. Along the ride, a recorded narration will give you some of the history and background of this amazing marvel. Your journey begins at the Valley Station at an elevation of 2,643 feet and ends at the Mountain Station at an elevation of 8,516 feet. You'll be transported to the Mount San Jacinto State Park, with 50 miles of hiking trails, ideal for picnicking and enjoying outdoor adventure. The Mountain Station offers two restaurants, a gift shop, and a terrace with awe-inspiring views.

Palm Springs Aerial Tramway
1 Tramway Road, Palm Springs
888-515-8726
pstramway.com

SCENIC ROAD TRIPS

One of the best ways to experience the natural beauty and diverse environment of the Greater Palm Springs region is from behind the wheel, and there are several notable scenic drives to choose from. Take Highway 10 to Highway 86 approximately 30 miles east out to the Salton Sea, the second-largest lake in California. The Salton Sea Recreation Area offers fishing, boating, camping, and excellent bird watching. Be sure to stop at the Visitors Center on the north side of the lake. Take the Palms to Pines Scenic Byway (Highway 74), an extraordinary 67-mile drive. Start out in Palm Desert on Highway 74; stop at the Vista Point for sweeping views, and continue on the road as it winds through forests and snow-capped mountains to the charming mountain village of Idyllwild, which is worth a visit.

Salton Sea State Recreation Area
100-225 State Park Road, Mecca
760-393-3052
parks.ca.gov/saltonsea

Palms to Pines Scenic Byway
Highway California 74
909-382-2600
fs.usda.gov/recarea/sbnf/recarea/?recid=26521

INSIDER'S TIP

If you want a scenic drive, definitely put the mountain arts community of Idyllwild on your list of things to do. From the desert cities of the Coachella Valley, Idyllwild is only an hour's drive but a world away. You can take one of two routes. Situated at an elevation of nearly 6,000 feet, Idyllwild offers a tranquil respite in a forest setting, with great hiking, dining, arts, music, shopping, and wine tasting at Middle Ridge Tasting Gallery.

idyllwild.com

WALK IN
ANCIENT FOOTSTEPS

When you visit Palm Springs, you may be surprised to realize you are on the site of a sovereign Indian nation. The Agua Caliente Band of Cahuilla Indians has inhabited the region for five centuries, and their 31,000-acre reservation extends to swaths of Palm Springs, Cathedral City, and portions of Rancho Mirage. The most significant sites on the reservation are Indian Canyons, four distinct canyons—Palm Canyon, Murray Canyon, Andreas Canyon, and Tahquitz Canyon. They offer thoroughly sublime scenery where you can hike among streams, pools, waterfalls, and the world's largest fan palm oasis. Indian Canyons are listed on the National Registry of Historic Places and are considered sacred land by this tribe, which requires respectful use of the canyons.

Indian Canyons
38500 South Palm Canyon Drive, Palm Springs
760-323-6018
indian-canyons.com

MEET ME
AT THE OASIS

Before the railroad, the site of the Thousand Palms Oasis at the Coachella Valley Preserve was a major stagecoach stop between the Colorado River gold mines and Los Angeles in the 1860s. Today the Thousand Palms Oasis, situated in the 18,000-acre Coachella Valley Preserve System, is a great recreational outpost with picnicking, guided tours, and more than 25 miles of hiking trails. Besides seeing a variety of rare habitats, you'll discover the preserve's fascinating geological and anthropological history. Inhabited by various Indian cultures for centuries, the preserve has cool ponds and springs that are fed from the famed San Andreas earthquake fault, which you can visit on a guided tour. Be sure to stop at the historic Palm House Visitors Center, a 1930s–40s rustic building that contains educational information about the natural and historic features of the area.

Thousand Palms Oasis/Coachella Valley Preserve
29200 Thousand Palms Canyon Road, Thousand Palms
760-343-2733
coachellavalleypreserve.org

FUN FACT

You'll see a large variety of palm trees throughout the Coachella Valley, but the palms that are present in the region's natural oases are *Washingtonia filifera,* commonly referred to as the California fan palm. Among 2,500 species of the world's palms, the fan palm is the only palm native to California.

A RIVER RUNS
THROUGH IT

The Whitewater Preserve is a pristine scenic riparian habitat on 2,800 acres located just northwest of Palm Springs. Under the aegis of the Wildlands Conservancy, the Whitewater Preserve is adjacent to the San Gorgonio Wilderness and is home to many native flora and fauna species. The Whitewater River will soon be designated a National Wild and Scenic River, pending legislation. Whitewater Preserve and its environs are open daily for hiking, picnicking, permit camping, and catch-and-release fishing with permit. There is a Visitor and Ranger Station with informational and educational materials to enhance your visit, such as trail maps, lists of flowers, birds, and reptile and amphibian species you may be able to spot. For seasoned hikers, there is a trail head connecting to the Pacific Crest Trail.

Whitewater Preserve
9160 Whitewater Canyon Road, Whitewater
760-325-7222
wildlandsconservancy.org/preserve_whitewater

MARCO
POLO

Poolside recreation in Greater Palm Springs is practically a religion, and it's a focal point for both visitors and residents alike. While all hotels and inns have a swimming pool, you have some other options for taking a dip, namely some public pools. Visitors can drop in at their leisure to enjoy these facilities: the Palm Desert Aquatic Center is an eight-acre facility at the Palm Desert Civic Park. It's operated by the City of Palm Desert and has three pools for lap swimming and swim and fitness classes, as well as water polo. The Palm Springs Swim Center features an Olympic-sized outdoor pool for year-round lap swimming, recreational swimming, and aquatic programs for all ages. The Swim Center is located adjacent to the city-operated Leisure Center.

Palm Desert Aquatic Center
73751 Magnesia Falls Drive, Palm Desert
760-565-7467
cityofpalmdesert.org/departments/parks-recreation/aquatic-center

Palm Springs Swim Center
405 S. Pavilion Way, Palm Springs
760-323-8278
palmspringsca.gov/government/departments/parks-recreation/swim-center

46

VENTURE
INTO THE ABYSS

Take one of the many San Andreas Fault tours to see California's fabled earthquake fault that inspires such enormous fascination. This geological wonder, which dates back 28 million years, traverses the length of the Coachella Valley and is an intriguing attraction. Tours to the legendary fault, offered by several tour operators, are guided excursions in either closed or open-air Jeeps and Hummers. Tour guides are naturalists who are knowledgeable about the geology, history, and flora and fauna of the area. You'll see 2-billion-year-old canyons that have been twisted over time by Mother Nature. Be sure to check the websites for a list of things to take along on your Jeep excursion.

Desert Adventures Red Jeep Tours
74794 Lennon Place, Palm Desert
760-324-5337
red-jeep.com

Big Wheel Tours
74850 42nd Avenue, Palm Desert
760-779-1837
bwbtours.com

TAKE A WALK
ON THE WILD SIDE

For a fun day communing with the natural world, enjoy an adventure at Palm Desert's The Living Desert Gardens & Zoo, which emphasizes education, conservation, and preservation. Established in 1970, The Living Desert has grown to 1,200 acres, of which 1,000 acres are a preserve featuring an undeveloped area of Sonoran desert in its natural state. Walk along the nature trails to see more than 450 animals from Africa, Australia, and North America. There are live animal shows, tram rides, sprawling gardens, exhibits, and a model train exhibit. The botanical gardens represent plants from the Southern California desert as well as from other regions of the world. The Living Desert also offers cafés, food concessions, gift shops, and a garden center where you can purchase rare plants.

The Living Desert Gardens & Zoo
47900 Portola Avenue, Palm Desert
760-346-5694
livingdesert.org

48

STAR
GAZING

The absence of big city lights in the desert region makes it ideal for stargazing. In nearby Joshua Tree National Park, you will find some of the darkest skies in Southern California, which allow awe-inspiring views of the Milky Way, constellations, planets, and, during certain times of the year, spectacular meteor showers. The National Park Service at Joshua Tree offers nighttime stargazing throughout the year. In celebration of the one hundredth anniversary of the National Park Service in 2016, Joshua Tree began a Night Sky Festival; call or check the website for more info. The Gargan Optics Observatory is a private, state-of-the-art, climate-controlled observatory that offers group stargazing shows by reservation. Experience the thrill of peering at the cosmos through a massive, research-grade, GPS-guided robotic telescope. Open Thursday through Sunday.

Joshua Tree National Park
74485 National Park Drive, Twentynine Palms
760-367-5500
nps.gov/jotr/planyourvisit/stargazing

Gargan Optics Observatory
72727 Jack Kramer Lane, Indio
760-238-4584

THE SPORT
OF KINGS

Polo in the desert? We've got that, too. In fact there has been world-class polo in the Coachella Valley for more than 50 years at two renowned polo clubs—the El Dorado Polo Club and the Empire Polo Club, both in Indio. During the season, from January to April, you can watch professional polo games that are open to the public every Sunday. Parking is $10, but admission for the polo games is free. You can purchase food and beverages or make it a fun tailgate picnic. At El Dorado you can enjoy a meal or drinks while watching the polo games from the Clubhouse or the Cantina. Polo is fast-paced and thrilling to watch; the games are held on an enormous verdant green field the size of nine football fields.

El Dorado Polo Club
50950 Madison Street, Indio
760-342-2223
eldoradopoloclub.com

Empire Polo Club
81800 Avenue 51, Indio
760-342-2762
empirepolo.com

INSIDER'S TIP

The Empire Polo Club is also site of the annual Coachella Valley Music and Arts Festival, the largest music festival in the world, which is held over two weekends in April. The free Sunday polo games are suspended at the beginning of April to accommodate the more than 200,000 attendees of Coachella.

STEP INTO
A VORTEX

A short 20-minute drive from Joshua Tree, a visit to the Integratron will reward you with the unique experience of a "sound bath" in an "acoustically perfect" dome sited on a powerful geomagnetic vortex. The Integratron was designed and built in the 1950s by George Van Tassel, a UFO theorist, to enhance rejuvenation, anti-gravity, and time travel, supposedly from instructions he received from visitors from the planet Venus. How's that for quirkiness? The Integratron was financed by donations, including funds from another eccentric, Howard Hughes. Under the present ownership, the Integratron is open for "sound baths" in the sound chamber while a sequence of quartz crystal singing bowls, which are keyed to the body's energy centers, are played. Visits are by reservation only, but you can bring a picnic to enjoy the grounds.

Integratron
2477 Belfield Boulevard, Landers
760-364-3126
integratron.com

INSIDER'S TIP

If vortices are your thing, the city of Desert Hot Springs is known to have numerous locations which are attributed to the convergence of five energies: earthquake faults, geothermal underground water, mountain peak alignments, wind, and sun energies. The city is also renowned for its hot springs spas. So if you don't encounter a vortex, you can rejuvenate your spirit in the city's many natural hot springs.

CHASE
THE WIND

You've likely seen all the windmills on the western edge of Palm Springs, but you can view them up close and personal on a Windmill Tour. The 90-minute to 2-hour tour takes you inside the gates of the private property where scores of operating windmills are located. Palm Springs Windmill Tours has headquarters on the site, where you can view a gallery of historic photos. The tour also includes an outdoor exhibit of various windmill designs of the past 35 years, and you'll learn why some were successful and others not so much. You'll get an interesting overview of the sustainable wind energy industry and other forms of alternative energy, including solar and natural gas. The tours are conducted with a knowledgeable guide in an enclosed, air-conditioned passenger van.

Palm Springs Windmill Tours
62950 20th Avenue, Palm Springs
760-770-2701
windmilltours.com

FUN FACT

The San Gorgonio Pass, located to the west of Palm Springs, is considered one of the windiest places in Southern California, creating an ideal location for the windmill industry, which explains why so many windmills dot the surrounding landscape.

VISIT NEW
NATIONAL MONUMENTS

After a 10-year effort by U.S. Senator Dianne Feinstein, Greater Palm Springs now boasts three new national monuments. In 2016, President Obama designated the Sand to Snow National Monument, Castle Mountains National Monument, and Mojave Trails National Monument, and in so doing, he protected an additional 1.8 million acres of diverse natural habitat that now create an unbroken corridor for many animal species, including bighorn sheep, tortoises, and fringe-toed lizards. Because the monuments cover a sweeping area, you can access them in various locations. The three monuments contain volcanic spires, dunes, ribbons of wetlands wedged between steep canyon walls, grasslands, Joshua tree forests, ancient petroglyphs, and the historic Route 66. Check the website for specific access points and recreational areas.

Sand to Snow National Monument
Castle Mountains National Monument
Mojave Trails National Monument
nps.gov/archeology/sites/antiquities/monumentslist.htm

SAY AHHHH!

If you like to pamper yourself and luxuriate in special spa treatments, you've come to the right place. There is such a variety of fabulous spas throughout the Coachella Valley, you'll be like a kid in a candy store looking for a sugar fix. One notable spa is the historic Two Bunch Palms, famous for its hot artesian waters that have healing properties derived from the lithium-rich hot springs. These hot waters in the resort's grotto originate from an ancient geothermal aquifer first noted by U.S. railroad surveyors in the late 1880s. Set on 77 picturesque acres, Two Bunch Palms has more than 80 rooms, a farm-to-table restaurant, a lap pool, and a full menu of spa services, which are available for either overnight or day-use guests.

Two Bunch Palms
67425 Two Bunch Palms Trail, Desert Hot Springs
760-329-8791
twobunchpalms.com

54

TEE TIME
IN THE DESERT

Considered a golfer's paradise, the Coachella Valley has you covered whether you're an avid or occasional golfer. With more than 120 golf courses and resorts, you won't find yourself far from a green. To keep up your golf swing, check out these top public courses. Westin Mission Hills offers two stellar courses the Pete Dye Resort Course and the Gary Player Signature Course, both top-caliber championship courses. Indian Wells Golf Resort completed an $80 million renovation to make the Celebrity Course and the Player Course the ultimate golf experiences. Desert Willow Golf Resort's Mountain View Course is a municipal golf course owned by the City of Palm Desert, with all the amenities of a top private facility. The Indian Canyons Golf Resort's South Course has spellbinding views of Mount San Jacinto.

Pete Dye Course and
Gary Player Signature Course,
Westin Mission Hills Resort
Rancho Mirage
for Pete Dye Course: 760-770-2908
for Gary Player Course: 760-328-3198
westinmissionhills.com

Celebrity Course and The Player Course,
Indian Wells Golf Resort
Indian Wells
760-346-4653
indianwellsresort.com

Mountain View Course, Desert Willow Golf Resort
Palm Desert
760-346-7060
desertwillow.com

South Course, Indian Canyons Golf Resort
Palm Springs
760-833-8700
indiancanyonsgolf.com

55

WATCH
THE PROS

If you prefer golf as a spectator sport, the Greater Palm Springs area has a long history of playing host to some of the country's most prestigious professional golf tournaments, not to mention the bold-faced names that have enjoyed the links in the Coachella Valley, including former President Dwight D. Eisenhower, Bob Hope, Frank Sinatra, President Bill Clinton, President Barack Obama, and many others. While most of the original tournament names have changed over the years with new title sponsors, there are many tournaments throughout the season where you can observe the world's best pro golfers mix it up with celebrities. Here are just a few annual tourneys:

The **CareerBuilder Challenge** (in January), formerly the Bob Hope Classic, but still continues Bob Hope's legacy of raising funds for local charities.
careerbuilderchallenge.com

The **Frank Sinatra Celebrity Invitational** (in February) was founded in 1986 by Sinatra to benefit the Barbara Sinatra Children's Center.
franksinatracelebritygolf.org

LPGA ANA Inspiration (in March/April), one of five major LPGA events, was formerly the Dinah Shore/Kraft Nabisco Championship.
anainspiration.com

YOGA
ON THE GREAT LAWN

There's no reason to forgo your yoga practice while visiting Coachella Valley. Head to Sunnylands Center & Gardens for a free hour-long class held on the expansive verdant lawn each Friday morning during the season. These free yoga classes are conducted by Kristin Olson, a respected yoga instructor for nearly 40 years. Held on Sunnylands' Great Lawn, the classes are suitable for all levels. You can't help being inspired by the outdoor setting surrounded by spectacular gardens and magnificent views of the soaring Mount San Jacinto. But if you miss these Friday yoga classes, you can still get in some exercise by walking the 1.25 miles of walking trails that meander through Sunnylands' sublime gardens.

Yoga at Sunnylands Center & Gardens
37977 Bob Hope Drive, Rancho Mirage
760-202-2222
sunnylands.org

PEDALING
FOR CHARITY

The Tour de Palm Springs, an annual signature cycling event in Palm Springs since 1999, draws 8,000 riders and 25,000 spectators from around the country. Held in January/February each year, the Tour de Palm Springs raises funds for several charities. Sponsored by Coachella Valley Serving People In Need (CVSPIN), this cycling event has raised more than $3 million as of 2016. The two-day event offers riders a choice of ride lengths—5, 10, 25, 50, or 100 miles. Walkers may also participate in 1.5- or 3-mile routes. The routes take riders throughout the streets of Palm Springs and through surrounding scenic areas. The event also features a vendor expo in downtown Palm Springs.

Tour de Palm Springs
74854 Velie Way, Suite 9, Palm Desert
760-674-4700
tourdepalmsprings.com

UP, UP, AND AWAY

The Cathedral City Hot Air Balloon Festival began in 2015 but quickly became a popular event for family-friendly fun. Held in February to coincide with Valentine's Day, the Balloon Festival hosts three days of activities that take place in various locations and venues, including Cathedral City's Civic Park. The festival features balloon tether rides, special event dinners, musical entertainment, gourmet food trucks, and a Kids' Zone. A highlight is the nighttime balloon glow event, with nearly 30 hot air balloons that are lit up to music during a 45-minute show. General admission to the festival is free; however, tickets and/or passes are required to participate in certain activities and access VIP areas. The event is organized by Fantasy Balloon Flights which operates balloon rides from October-May if you miss the event in February.

Cathedral City Hot Air Balloon Festival—Cathedral City Civic Park
68700 Avenida Lalo Guerrero, Cathedral City
(check website for dates and other locations)
hotairballoonfest.com

Fantasy Balloon Fights
800-569-0997
fantasyballoonflight.com

THE PEOPLE PARADE

One of the most popular activities in Greater Palm Springs is the sport of people-watching—and it's absolutely free. In fact, people-watching is a very popular sport, particularly along Palm Canyon Drive in downtown Palm Springs, which is ground zero for superb people-watching opportunities. To snag a front-row seat for the "people parade," head to any number of the pubs, bistros, and eateries with relaxing outdoor patios that dot Palm Canyon Drive. Here are just a few:

Alibi Azul
369 N. Palm Canyon Drive,
Palm Springs
760-325-5533
alibiazul.com

Joey Palm Springs
245 S. Palm Canyon Drive,
Palm Springs
760-320-8370
joeyps.com

Lulu California Bistro
200 S. Palm Canyon Drive,
Palm Springs
760-327-5858
lulupalmsprings.com

Peabody's Coffee Bar
134 S. Palm Canyon Drive,
Palm Springs
760-322-1877
peabodyscafepalmsprings.com

Trio
707 N. Palm Canyon Drive,
Palm Springs
760-864-8746
triopalmsprings.com

Zin American Bistro
198 S. Palm Canyon Drive,
Palm Springs
760-322-6300
pszin.com

OUTBACK
ADVENTURE

Venture off the beaten path with Adventure Hummer Tours to see the mesmerizing desert landscape up close and personal. You'll be in for an off-roading adventure in an open-air H1 Hummer or an enclosed luxurious H2 Hummer with military-grade suspension for a smooth ride. The company offers several tours to many destinations including Joshua Tree National Park, which includes lunch or dinner for a value-added experience. The adventure tours to Joshua Tree take you a mile high in the back country, where you can see ancient rock formations, a variety of animal life, and the world-famous Joshua trees, which can live to be 1,000 years old. Adventure Hummer Tours can accommodate private groups or corporate groups of any size.

Adventure Hummer Tours
760-285-0876
adventurehummer.com

TAKE TO
THE SKIES

Experience the thrill of flying in a restored vintage 1940 Stearman biplane for an unparalleled bird's-eye view of the Coachella Valley. Palm Springs Biplanes offers thrilling open-cockpit rides for one or two persons. The tours—the 15-minute Barnstormer, the 30-minute Coachella Coaster, or the one-hour Southern Cross—fly over different portions of the Coachella Valley's picturesque desert and mountain landscape. Palm Springs Biplanes can even arrange to document your flight with a digitally recorded video as a special keepsake.

Palm Springs Biplanes
760-216-3700
psbiplanes.com

BE A
ROCK STAR

Want to test your endurance and stamina? Prove your mettle at Desert Rocks Indoor Climbing Gym for an exhilarating adventure. It's both a gym and a place for recreational fun that is suitable for all ages and fitness levels. The facility has 7,000 square feet of space with two 28-foot walls for harness climbing in the main room. There is also a 17-foot bouldering wall for unharnessed climbing, but don't worry, there is a foam pad underneath for your safety. A second room, available for private events, features another wall for beginning climbers. It's open seven days a week year-round, so even during the summer months you can enjoy an indoor rock climbing experience in an air-conditioned environment. Yoga and fitness classes are also available.

Desert Rocks Indoor Climbing Gym
19160 McLane Street, Desert Hot Springs
760-671-1101
climbdesertrocks.com

63

RIDE
THE WAVES

Palm Springs might be about 100 miles from the Pacific Ocean, but you can still experience a little of the California surf lifestyle at Wet 'n Wild Palm Springs, a large water park with a variety of rides for all ages. Enjoy a bit of the California Dreamin' surf lifestyle with Wet 'n Wild's FlowRider, which simulates perfect surf waves. Try the Pipeline with its three slides—an open-body slide, an open-tube slide, and an enclosed-body slide. Or check out the thrill of the gravity-defying speed slides of the Tidal Wave Towers, which are seven stories high. Kahuna's Beach House is a four-story family fun house with interactive water jets and more. Private cabanas, food concessions, and wading pools for tots make this great family fun from March-October.

Wet 'n Wild Palm Springs
1500 S. Gene Autry Trail, Palm Springs
760-327-0499
wetnwildpalmsprings.com

LADY
LUCK

Try your luck in one of Coachella Valley's many gaming casinos, where you'll find Las Vegas–style gaming. There are several glamorous casinos on sovereign tribal reservations with hotels, dining, and entertainment, plus slot machines and a variety of table games. On the east end of the valley, Spotlight 29 Casino features 1,600 slot machines, plus five-dollar tables and slot and blackjack tournaments. Just down the road you'll find Fantasy Springs Resort Casino with 2,000 slot machines, video poker, and 40 table games. In mid-valley is the Agua Caliente Casino Resort Spa, where you can enjoy slots, table games, a high-limit room, and a poker room. In downtown Palm Springs at the Spa Resort Casino, you'll be able to enjoy gaming 24/7 with slots, table games, and more.

Spotlight 29 Casino
46200 Harrison Place, Coachella
760-775-5566
spotlight29.com

Fantasy Springs Resort Casino
84245 Indio Springs Drive, Indio
760-342-5000
fantasyspringsresort.com

Agua Caliente Casino
32250 Bob Hope Drive,
Rancho Mirage
888-999-1995
hotwatercasino.com

Spa Resort Casino
401 E. Amado Road, Palm Springs
888-999-1995
sparesortcasino.com

AN ANCIENT LAKE

For a fun family- and pet-friendly outing, check out the Lake Cahuilla Recreation Area, a 710-acre recreational site that offers lots of outdoor adventure. The lake's origin has been traced to the Pleistocene glacial age when the Colorado River created freshwater lakes in the region. The lake was almost 100 miles long by 35 miles across at its widest point. Situated at the foot of the Santa Rosa Mountains, Lake Cahuilla's adjacent hillsides still show evidence of the ancient shorelines. Today, Lake Cahuilla is a popular spot for camping, hiking, fishing, picnicking, and swimming. There's even an annual Trout Fishing Derby. The recreation area is open year-round, but check the website, as some of these activities are only available at specific times of the year.

Lake Cahuilla Recreation Area
58075 Jefferson Street, La Quinta
760-564-4712
rivcoparks.org/parks/lake-cahuilla

RELIVE
THE WILD WEST

Just a 32-mile scenic drive from Palm Springs is a slice of the Old West at Pioneertown, an authentic Hollywood creation of a Western town that was built in 1946. Pioneertown is a perfectly preserved full-scale town built as a motion picture set. The town comprises several rustic structures, including a corral, a marshal's office, a church, and other façades as well as a working post office and shops. The Pioneertown Motel, originally built to house actors and crew, can be rented for overnight stays so you can check in and stay a spell. Pioneertown served as a set and backdrop for numerous television shows and Western films, including *The Cisco Kid*, the 1950s TV show. Pioneertown has a few shops and hosts shoot-out reenactments. Don't miss Pappy & Harriet's Pioneertown Palace for great grub and live music.

Pioneertown Motel
5040 Curtis Road, Pioneertown
760-365-7001
visitpalmsprings.com/overview/play/pioneertown

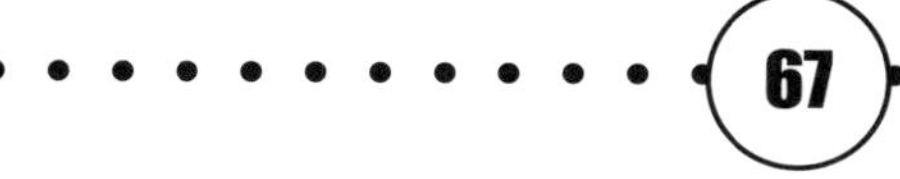

GIDDY
UP

If you're hankering for a bit of the cowboy way, Smoke Tree Stables can put you in the saddle again. Palm Springs had a robust equestrian culture in its early days, and Smoke Tree Stables has been organizing trail rides since 1927. The stables are located adjacent to 150 miles of scenic trails that allow riders to experience the serenity and the beauty of the desert landscape up close. Individual or group rides for all levels of experience are available for either hourly or day rides. Day rides can include a tasty picnic or a cowboy cookout. Trail rides will take you into the pristine habitat of the local mountains and the Indian Canyons, located on sacred ancestral tribal lands, where you will encounter historic palm oases and year-round cool streams. Please note that Smoke Tree Stables is closed in July and August.

Smoke Tree Stables
2500 S. Toledo Avenue, Palm Springs
760-327-1372
smoketreestables.com

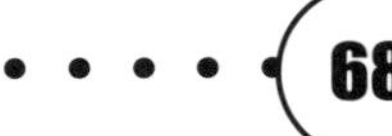

TAKE
A HIKE

Greater Palm Springs is renowned for its diverse hiking opportunities throughout the Coachella Valley, with 140 trails that traverse over 1,250 miles. The climate during the season (October through May) is ideal for getting outdoors and enjoying our magnificent landscape and awe-inspiring beauty. A good source for some of the best hiking trails is Desert Trails Hiking Club. You can join them on their hikes for an annual fee of $10 for one or $15 for two or a family, which also gives you a membership in their club. The Coachella Valley Hiking Club also organizes several hikes per week that vary from easy to moderate to strenuous. Check the hike schedule and register for hikes on their websites. You can also get information about hiking trails from the Palm Springs Bureau of Tourism.

Coachella Valley Hiking Club
cvhikingclub.net

Desert Trails Hiking Club
deserthikingtrails.com

Palm Springs Bureau of Tourism
visitpalmsprings.com

INSIDER'S TIP

Be aware that the desert climate and landscape can be harsh and requires mindfulness and preparation. Follow these simple guidelines and you'll have a richly rewarding experience: Stay on designated trails so you won't get lost. Be sure to have plenty of water, snacks, sunscreen, proper footwear, and a charged cell phone for emergencies. In summer months, hike in the morning and avoid the hottest part of the day.

Double-decker Architecture Bus Tours
Photo Credit:
Greater Palm Springs CVB

CULTURE AND HISTORY

ANCIENT HISTORY, VIBRANT CULTURE

Palm Springs has a rich Native American history that dates back at least 2,000 years. The Agua Caliente Band of Cahuilla Indians, whose ancestral home has been Palm Springs and neighboring regions for centuries, still plays an active and dynamic role in the community. Their history is skillfully documented with changing exhibitions at the Agua Caliente Cultural Museum. Housed in an intimate space on the Village Green in the heart of downtown Palm Springs, the ACCM is affiliated with the Smithsonian Institution, giving the museum a mighty stature despite being small. In addition to exhibitions, the museum presents numerous programs such as lectures, hikes, and demonstrations. The Agua Caliente Cultural Museum inspires people to learn about the Agua Caliente Band of Cahuilla Indians and other native cultures through its exhibitions, collections, research, and educational programs.

Agua Caliente Cultural Museum
219 S. Palm Canyon Drive, Palm Springs
760 323-0151
accmuseum.org

A QUIRKY
LEGACY

One of the most unusual museums you're likely to see anywhere is Cabot's Pueblo Museum, a rambling pueblo-style dwelling of 35 rooms that was the homesteaded residence of a stalwart pioneer named Cabot Yerxa. Located in the hills of Desert Hot Springs, Cabot's Pueblo Museum is a fascinating architectural marvel that Cabot built largely by hand from repurposed and recycled materials during a period of more than 20 years. Before he homesteaded 160 desolate acres in 1913, Cabot Yerxa was a citizen of the world, traveling to Cuba, Mexico, and Alaska and studying art in France. He was also a devoted advocate of Native Americans. Take a docent-led tour to learn about this intriguing visionary and see the collection of rare objects he amassed during his world travels.

Cabot's Pueblo Museum
67616 E. Desert View Drive, Desert Hot Springs
760-329-7610

71

A CULTURAL
TRIO

One of the oldest cultural institutions in the desert is the Palm Springs Art Museum, which was founded in 1938, the same year as the city of Palm Springs itself. Visitors are frequently surprised to find a world-class museum in our small resort town. The 125,000-square-foot museum has a noteworthy art collection and presents exceptional and engaging exhibitions throughout the year. PSAM houses two outdoor sculpture gardens, a café, and the renowned Annenberg Theater, which presents a variety of performing arts. Under its cultural umbrella, PSAM has two other entities—the Architecture & Design Center, Edwards Harris Pavilion, in downtown Palm Springs, and the Palm Springs Art Museum, Palm Desert – The Galen, with its four-acre Faye Sarkowsky Sculpture Garden.

Palm Springs Art Museum
101 Museum Drive, Palm Springs
760-322-4800

Architecture & Design Center
300 S. Palm Canyon Drive, Palm Springs
760-423-5260

The Galen, Palm Springs Art Museum, Palm Desert
72567 Highway 111 at El Paseo, Palm Desert
760-346-5600
psmuseum.org

INSIDER'S TIP

The Palm Springs Art Museum hosts Free Thursdays from 4 p.m. to 8 p.m., while the other two museums—the Architecture & Design Center in Palm Springs and The Galen in Palm Desert—are free daily. The free admission policy may continue depending upon special underwriting; check the website or call. The Galen's Faye Sarkowsky Sculpture Garden is free and open year-round; download a guide for a self-guided garden tour.

ART OFF
THE BEATEN PATH

Discover a small but dynamic enclave of artist-owned galleries and working studios at the Backstreet Art District, located off the beaten path on a side street from East Palm Canyon Drive. You'll find a vibrant art scene and original works in a variety of media, including paintings, ceramics, jewelry, sculpture, and photography, all in one location. Stop in during the Backstreet Art District's monthly Art Walk on the first Wednesday of each month during the "season." The Art Walk is a convivial evening that takes place from 6 p.m. to 9 p.m. and gives you an opportunity to meet and chat with the artists, visit working studios, and enjoy refreshments while perusing (and possibly buying) high-quality works of art.

Backstreet Art District
2600 South Cherokee Way, Palm Springs
backstreetartdistrict.com

WALK THROUGH HISTORY

Take one of Palm Springs Historical Society's nine seasonal Historic Walking Tours to hear entertaining tales of intrigue about Palm Springs's glamorous history, culture, architecture, and local tribal legacy. You'll also learn interesting stories about many of the celebrities who made their home here. The tours take you on a casual stroll through some notable and historic neighborhoods and portions of the town with a knowledgeable docent who will regale you with fascinating tidbits about local lore and celebrities who have lived, loved, and played in the Palm Springs oasis. The tours are offered during the "season" (October through April).

P.S. Walk With Me also offers walking tours curated by lifelong local resident Jade Nelson for groups of two to 12.

Historic Walking Tours
Palm Springs Historical Society, 221 S. Palm Canyon Drive, Palm Springs
760-323-8297
pshistoricalsociety.org

P.S. Walk With Me
855-955-9255
pswalk.com

ART ON
PARADE

In the City of Palm Desert, you'll find more than 150 works of public art throughout the city. As part of the city's Art in Public Places program, you'll see paintings, water features, and sculptures by renowned and local professional artists. You can enjoy a self-guided tour at your convenience or join a free docent-led public art tour one Saturday a month from September through May. Private tours for groups of more than three persons can also be scheduled. Along El Paseo, Palm Desert's lively shopping corridor, you will find several blocks of large-scale public art sculptures. Drop in to the Visitors Center to get started or you can view and print a map of all the public art from the city's website—a handy way to help you navigate around the city to enjoy this stunning collection.

Art in Public Places—Palm Desert Visitor Services
73-510 Fred Waring Drive, Palm Desert
800-873-2428 or 760-568-1441
palm-desert.org/arts-culture/public-art

75

THE LANGUAGE
OF FILM

For a region the size of Greater Palm Springs, the number of film festivals hosted here rivals that of most major metropolitan cities. The highest profile is the Palm Springs International Film Festival, held each January. It began in 1990 and has since garnered the esteem and respect of the film industry as being a reliable source for handicapping Oscar® winners. The 10-day PSIFF presents upwards of 200 international films; in addition, it's one of the only places you can view all of the Foreign Language Academy Award nominees. The PSIFF black-tie gala draws an impressive roster of A-list actors whose films are in contention for Oscar® consideration. The PSIFF is presented under the auspices of the Palm Springs International Film Society, which hosts screenings and events throughout the year.

Palm Springs International Film Festival
Festival office: 1700 E. Tahquitz Canyon Way, Suite 3, Palm Springs
760-322-2930 or 800-898-7256
psfilmfest.org

76

MORE CINEMATIC CELEBRATIONS

If you miss the Palm Springs International Film Festival in January, not to worry—there are several other specialty film festivals throughout the year. The Palm Springs International Film Society presents the annual Palm Springs International ShortFest (June), the largest festival of its kind in the United States. The ShortFest focuses on a variety of media and genres, including action, comedies, documentaries, dramas, horror stories, thrillers, and mysteries. Cinema Diverse: The Palm Springs Gay & Lesbian Film Festival (September) takes place at The Camelot Theatres and presents the best in LGBT cinema. The Native FilmFest (March) is produced by the Agua Caliente Cultural Museum and showcases the best in films by, about, and starring Native Americans and other indigenous peoples from around the world.

Palm Springs International ShortFest
Festival office: 1700 E. Tahquitz Canyon Way, Suite 3, Palm Springs
760-322-2930 or 800-898-7256
psfilmfest.org

Cinema Diverse
760-880-4921
cinemadiverse.org

Native FilmFest
760-778-1079
accmuseum.org

ART, MUSIC,
AND FOOD

The climate and clarity of light have long been reasons so many artists have found artistic inspiration in the stark beauty of the desert landscape. These factors have resulted in a dynamic and exciting art environment in Greater Palm Springs, which hosts numerous art events and festivals. The La Quinta Arts Foundation, founded in 1982, presents The La Quinta Arts Festival (March) which features three days of art exhibits, live entertainment, and wonderful food. You can see the artwork of more than 200 artists from around the United States and abroad. Check the website for dates.

La Quinta Arts Foundation
760-564-1244
lqaf.com

THE MORE ART
THE BETTER

Around the desert communities you'll find several other impressive and fun art events throughout the season. Most of the art events augment the visitor experience with live music in sunny outdoor settings held over two, three, or four days. The Rancho Mirage Art Affaire is a weekend celebration of art, food, and entertainment in November. The Southwest Arts Festival in January presents a three-day festival with nearly 300 artists. The Palm Springs Fine Art Fair, held in February, features galleries from around the country and abroad exhibiting modern and contemporary art in a variety of media. The Indian Wells Art Festival, a three-day juried art festival held in April, presents the work of 200 artists from around the world.

Rancho Mirage Art Affaire
Rancho Mirage Community Park,
71560 San Jacinto Drive, Rancho Mirage
760-324-4511
ranchomirageca.gov/art-affaire/

Southwest Arts Festival
Empire Polo Club,
81800 Avenue 51, Indio
760-347-0676
discoverindio.com/southwest-arts-festival

Palm Springs Fine Art Fair
Palm Springs Convention Center,
277 N. Avenida Caballeros, Palm Springs
800-563-7632
art-palmsprings.com

Indian Wells Art Festival
Indian Wells Tennis Garden,
78200 Miles Avenue, Indian Wells
760-346-0042
indianwellsartsfestival.com

ARCHITECTURE
ON WHEELS

Learn about Palm Springs's historic midcentury modern architectural heritage through a privately guided tour. There are several to choose from and they all offer an excellent overview of the city's notable commercial and residential midcentury modern architecture. The tours are conducted for groups of six in comfortable, seven-passenger vehicles and range from 90 minutes to three hours. Each tour operator is exceptionally knowledgeable about the city's architecture and offers slightly different tours with an individual focus. Some tours are strictly exterior tours, while some offer interior tours of a couple of homes or buildings. But each will provide an illuminating and even entertaining overview of many of Palm Springs's architectural gems, and you'll learn some fascinating historical tidbits. Tours also highlight the homes of many film, music, and literary luminaries.

Palm Springs Modern Tours
760-318-6118
palmspringsmoderntours.com

The Modern Tour
760-904-0904
themoderntour.com

Mod Squad Architecture & Design Tours
760-469-9265
psmodsquad.com

INSIDER'S TIP

You can also download an app for a self-driving architecture tour of Palm Springs's modern architecture. The app is narrated by local architecture historians and has more than 80 architectural landmarks. Download the app at: http://palmspringslife.com/Palm-Springs-Life/Mobile-Apps/Mod-Com-Apps/

CAMP DAVID
OF THE WEST

The Annenberg Retreat at Sunnylands is a spectacular 200-acre site in Rancho Mirage that was the former private residence of the late power couple Walter and Leonore Annenberg. The Annenbergs were legendary for hosting presidents, royalty, and numerous heads of state. Today, Sunnylands carries on the Annenbergs' mission "to address serious issues facing the nation and the world community" by hosting diplomatic summits for present and future presidents. President Barack Obama convened several international diplomatic summits at Sunnylands. The Center & Gardens are free and open to the public Thursday through Sunday (September through June) and feature a theater, a gift store, and a café, as well as expansive postcard gardens, and host free exhibits, concerts, films, and Friday yoga classes. The 25,000 square foot Annenberg residence, a midcentury modern marvel built in 1966, is open for tours by reservation.

Sunnylands
37977 Bob Hope Drive, Rancho Mirage
760-202-2222
sunnylands.org

REMEMBERING
THE HOLOCAUST

Visit the Desert Holocaust Memorial, located at the City of Palm Desert's Civic Center Park, to view a moving tribute to Holocaust victims and survivors. This outdoor memorial is a place of remembrance created by artist Dee Clements to honor the children, parents, loved ones, and millions of innocent people whose lives were lost in the Holocaust. The centerpiece of the Holocaust Memorial features larger-than-life-sized sculptures and bas-reliefs that capture the heart-wrenching human tragedy that took place during the Holocaust at the hands of the Nazis. The memorial also features a pedestal with an urn containing the names of 12,000 brave souls who helped many Jews. The sculptures and the bas-reliefs depict the faces and details taken from actual photos and other archival materials from the Holocaust Museum in Washington, D.C.

Desert Holocaust Memorial—Palm Desert Civic Center Park
Fred Waring Drive & San Pablo Avenue
760-324-4737
palm-desert.org/arts-culture/public-art/art

INSIDER'S TIP

Greater Palm Springs, also referred to as the Coachella Valley, comprises nine distinct cities, each with its own attributes and history. As a result, you will find that Greater Palm Springs boasts several historical museums and historical societies that contain fascinating and colorful local history of their respective towns.

A LIVING
HISTORY

Since 1965, a dedicated group of volunteers of the Coachella Valley Historical Society has kept a large archive of local history including photographs, artifacts, and memorabilia, opening the Coachella Valley History Museum in 1984. Open from October 1 to May 31, the Coachella Valley History Museum is a slice of living history about the agricultural heritage and the development of the Coachella Valley. Each spring, the museum hosts a free annual Heritage Festival in Old Town Indio, with an antique car show, exhibits, food, and a variety of live entertainment. Visit the website for a calendar of special events and exhibits.

Coachella Valley History Museum
82626 Miles Avenue, Indio
760-342-6651
cvhm.org

FUN FACT

It's believed that the name of the region, "Coachella" Valley, was the result of a simple spelling error by early mapmakers for the Southern Pacific Railroad in the late 1880s. The original reference to the area was "Conchilla," meaning "seashell" in Spanish, named so because of the fossilized mollusk shells that lived in an ancient body of water; shells can still be found in the area. Despite the spelling error, the name Coachella stuck.

KEEPING CULTURE
ALIVE

The City of La Quinta is one of the only cities in the area that has grown up around a historic resort instead of the other way around. When the famed La Quinta Resort opened in 1926, it was located in a remote patch of desert with little population. This is chronicled at the La Quinta Museum, which is both a central repository for La Quinta's archival and historical collection and a main cultural center for the city's visitors and residents. The museum, which is open year-round and is operated by the City of La Quinta, hosts a variety of cultural events throughout the year. Grab a brown bag lunch and enjoy a recorded TED talk. Or attend a First Friday Concert, one of the museum's live music concerts. The museum also hosts book discussions with the Gallery Book Club, children's story time, and craft classes.

La Quinta Museum
77885 Avenida Montezuma, La Quinta
760-777-7170
la-quinta.org/your-government/community-services/museum

84

REMEMBERING
THE GREATEST GENERATION

For U.S. military and aviation history buffs, a visit to the Palm Springs Air Museum is a must. The Air Museum is a living history museum housed in three climate-controlled airplane hangars with more than 40 vintage World War II warbirds and rare Korean War and Vietnam-era airplanes; many are still operational. The museum has a theater and a café and also contains exhibits, photographs, and video footage that tell the history of America's military involvement during the Korean War, World War II, and the Vietnam War. Many of the volunteer docents are veterans of these wars. You also can experience the thrill of riding in one of their vintage C-47 Skytrain and P-51 Mustang warbirds. The Palm Springs Air Museum has been named one of the world's top aviation museums by CNN.

Palm Springs Air Museum
745 N. Gene Autry Trail, Palm Springs
760-778-6262
palmspringsairmuseum.org

THE MECCA
OF MODERNISM

The City of Palm Springs is world-renowned for its astonishing preponderance of midcentury modern architecture—structures that were built between the 1930s and the 1960s. In fact, Palm Springs boasts more midcentury modern architecture than any other place. To this end, the city celebrates its architectural heritage each year with Modernism Week. Held twice a year in October and February, Modernism Week annually draws more than 70,000 people from around the world. The 11-day festival in February features modernist design, architecture, fashion, and more. There are multiple home and garden tours, lectures, parties, films, the wildly popular Double Decker Architecture Bus Tours, and the Modernism Show & Sale which features more than 80 exhibitors. Many other cities in the Coachella Valley also participate. Check the website for dates, a list of events, and to purchase tickets.

Modernism Week
modernismweek.com

HISTORIC HOME
TOURS

Palm Springs not only has a celebrated architectural heritage, but it also has a rich and fascinating cultural history told through a tour of the historic O'Donnell House, which is listed on the National Registry of Historic Places. Enjoy a 90-minute docent-led tour of this extraordinary, meticulously restored home, built in 1925. The historical tour of the O'Donnell House, also known as *Ojo del Desierto,* or "Eye of the Desert," recounts the history of Palm Springs as seen from high on the hillside above the Palm Springs Art Museum. The house also features a fine collection of mission-style furnishings, including rare tiles, pottery, and early California furniture. The O'Donnell House was spotlighted in actress Diane Keaton's 2007 book *California Romantica,* which chronicled rare California Mission style and Spanish Colonial homes.

O'Donnell House
800-966-9597
odonnellhouse.com

KEEPERS
OF THE FLAME

Visit an authentic adobe structure that houses the Palm Springs Historical Society, which is located at downtown's Village Green, a collection of historic buildings and museums open for public tours. Since 1955, the PSHS has been the archival and curatorial keeper of Palm Springs's fascinating and colorful history. The Palm Springs Historical Society operates two of Palm Springs's oldest buildings—the McCallum Adobe, which was built in 1888 and houses the society's exhibits, and the Cornelia White House, built in 1893—both open for tours. You'll enjoy perusing historic photographs, rare archives, paintings, and changing exhibitions at the McCallum Adobe. You can also see a 20-minute film that will give you a quick overview of the town's nearly 80-year history. Both museums are free to the public and are open from October to May.

Palm Springs Historical Society
221 S. Palm Canyon Drive, Palm Springs
760-323-8297
pshistoricalsociety.org

HISTORIC
SPECIMENS

Take time to visit the enchanting historic grounds of Moorten Botanical Garden, which was a favorite Palm Springs attraction of the late Huell Howser, the PBS-TV host. The gardens were established by Chester "Cactus Slim" and Patricia Moorten in 1938, the same year the City of Palm Springs was founded. These early Palm Springs residents created a truly unique garden of 3,000 cacti and succulents, some of which are available for purchase. The botanical garden, now operated by their son, Clark Moorten, is situated on more than an acre, with walkways, water features, ancient fossils, and other historic relics throughout the meandering gardens. Don't miss what perhaps might be the world's only "cactarium," which features rare specimens from deserts around the world. The family home, a historic Spanish Mediterranean structure, is now used for private events and weddings.

Moorten Botanical Garden
1701 S. Palm Canyon Drive, Palm Springs
760-327-6555
moortenbotanicalgarden.com

INSIDER'S TIP

Watch for a new, exciting event to launch in Greater Palm Springs. Desert X—a three-month site-specific curated exhibition in outdoor and indoor locations throughout the region—will have its inaugural event February 23 through April 2017. Desert X will showcase the work of contemporary artists, writers, architects, and musicians who will create public works that are inspired by the desert landscape. Check the website for exhibitions, artists, and events.

desertx.org

Uptown Design District
Photo Credit:
Palm Springs
Bureau of Tourism

SHOPPING AND FASHION

UPTOWN
SHOPPING

Along a tony stretch of North Palm Canyon in Palm Springs is the Uptown Design District, a fun shopping and dining corridor. As the name implies, the Uptown Design District captures the zeitgeist of trendsetting fashions, stylish home décor, and collectible midcentury modern furnishings, as well as popular high-style eateries. The first of many Trina Turk Boutiques around the United States opened in the Uptown Design District in 2002 and helped launch her brand. The district runs along North Palm Canyon from Alejo Road north to Vista Chino Drive, a distance of a little more than a mile, which makes a visit to the Uptown Design District a very comfortable and walkable experience. Stop for lunch at any of the acclaimed restaurants, grab an excellent coffee, or treat yourself to a refreshing craft cocktail along the way.

Trina Turk Boutique
891 N. Palm Canyon Drive, Palm Springs
760-416-2856
trinaturk.com

ROCKING
THE RUNWAY

The annual Fashion Week El Paseo, held each March, is a highly anticipated signature event of the "season" in the Coachella Valley. Fashion Week El Paseo is the largest annual fashion event on the West Coast and features a week-long event of runway shows, receptions, after-parties, trunk shows, and meet-and-greet opportunities with former and present *Project Runway* designers. Since its inception more than 10 years ago, Fashion Week El Paseo, so-named for its location in the El Paseo shopping district in Palm Desert, has showcased the work of both renowned and emerging couture designers in nightly runway shows. Unlike other fashion weeks around the country and throughout the world, Fashion Week El Paseo is geared to the public. Check the website for dates and to purchase tickets.

Fashion Week El Paseo
For tickets: 888-596-1027
fashionweekelpaseo.com

SHOP RODEO DRIVE
OF THE DESERT

The El Paseo Shopping District in Palm Desert will please the most discriminating shopaholics with its mile-long boulevard and 300 shops. You'll be able to choose from a dizzying variety of boutiques and retailers specializing in jewelry, apparel, art, home décor, and more than two dozen restaurants and cafés. Nearly every luxury brand has a presence on El Paseo, including Tiffany & Co., Louis Vuitton, Burberry, Escada, St. John, Gucci, and Ralph Lauren. But modest budgets will also find reason to shop 'til you drop, with retailers like Chicos, Talbots, Banana Republic, and Tommy Bahama. The Gardens on El Paseo provide a relaxing respite in their beautifully landscaped gardens and courtyards which often feature live concerts. Check the website for a schedule of special events.

El Paseo Shopping District
palm-desert.org/things-to-do/shopping/el-paseo

AN OUTDOOR
BAZAAR

For more than 30 years, the College of the Desert Street Fair has been a favorite weekend tradition for residents and visitors alike. The COD Street Fair is a colorful and festive outdoor shopping bazaar held on the College of the Desert campus. You'll find more than 300 merchant and artist booths, live entertainment, gourmet food, and a farmers market in winter months. You'll have fun perusing a huge selection of offerings at great prices including clothing, art, furniture, pottery, jewelry, leather goods, home décor, pet accessories, crafts, and gourmet specialty items, plus plants and flowers. The COD Street Fair is open on Saturdays and Sundays year-round. From October through May hours are 7 a.m. to 2 p.m., and from June through September the hours are 7 a.m. to 12 noon.

College of the Desert Street Fair
43500 Monterey Avenue, Palm Desert
codaastreetfair.com

A VINTAGE MARKETPLACE

If you are a fan of retro, vintage, or midcentury modern style, the Palm Springs Vintage Market is for you. Held the first Sunday of the month from 8 a.m. to 2 p.m. (October through May) in the shaded parking area of Camelot Theatres, the Vintage Market is a fun, treasure-hunting experience. Vendor booths display a variety of wares, such as vintage clothing, jewelry, home furnishings, toys and collectibles, furniture, records, and assorted retro memorabilia. Spend a leisurely morning perusing retro *objets d'art* while enjoying live music and meeting friendly folks who share your interest in the unusual and rare. Camelot Theatres' café offers a menu of breakfast and lunch selections, coffee, tea, and soft drinks to fortify yourself while shopping.

Palm Springs Vintage Market
Camelot Theatres, 2300 E. Baristo Road, Palm Springs
760-534-7968
palmspringsvintagemarket.com

IT TAKES
A VILLAGE

The historic town of Palm Springs is proud of its small-village feel. Every Thursday evening, you can celebrate VillageFest when the main downtown thoroughfare, Palm Canyon Drive, is closed to vehicular traffic for several blocks (from Baristo Road to Amado Road). VillageFest is a city event that celebrated its twenty-fifth anniversary in 2016 and has been a weekly year-round tradition for locals and visitors who flock downtown for the festival atmosphere. You can shop for handcrafted art, gift items, and fresh produce. There are also lots of food concessions and live music, creating a lively family- and dog-friendly event. VillageFest takes place 6 p.m. to 10 p.m. from October through May and 7 p.m. to 10 p.m. June through September.

VillageFest
villagefest.org

BARGAIN
HUNTING

Just 20 minutes east of Palm Springs you'll find the Desert Hills Premium Outlets, ground zero for fashionistas and home to the largest collection of luxury outlets in California. Desert Hills is located in Cabazon, where you can shop at nearly 200 designer outlets, such as Alexander McQueen, Dolce & Gabbana, Gucci, Helmut Lang, Jimmy Choo, Neiman Marcus Last Call, Polo Ralph Lauren Factory Store, Prada, Saint Laurent Paris, Saks Fifth Avenue OFF 5TH, Salvatore Ferragamo, Versace, and many more. Take a break from your bargain shopping at the food courts or nearby restaurants and the famous Hadley Fruit Orchards, a roadside institution since 1951. Desert Hills Premium Outlets are open Monday through Saturday from 10 a.m. to 9 p.m. and Sunday 10 a.m. to 8 p.m.

Desert Hills Premium Outlets
48400 Seminole Drive, Cabazon
951-849-5018 or 951-849-6641
premiumoutlets.com/outlet/desert-hills

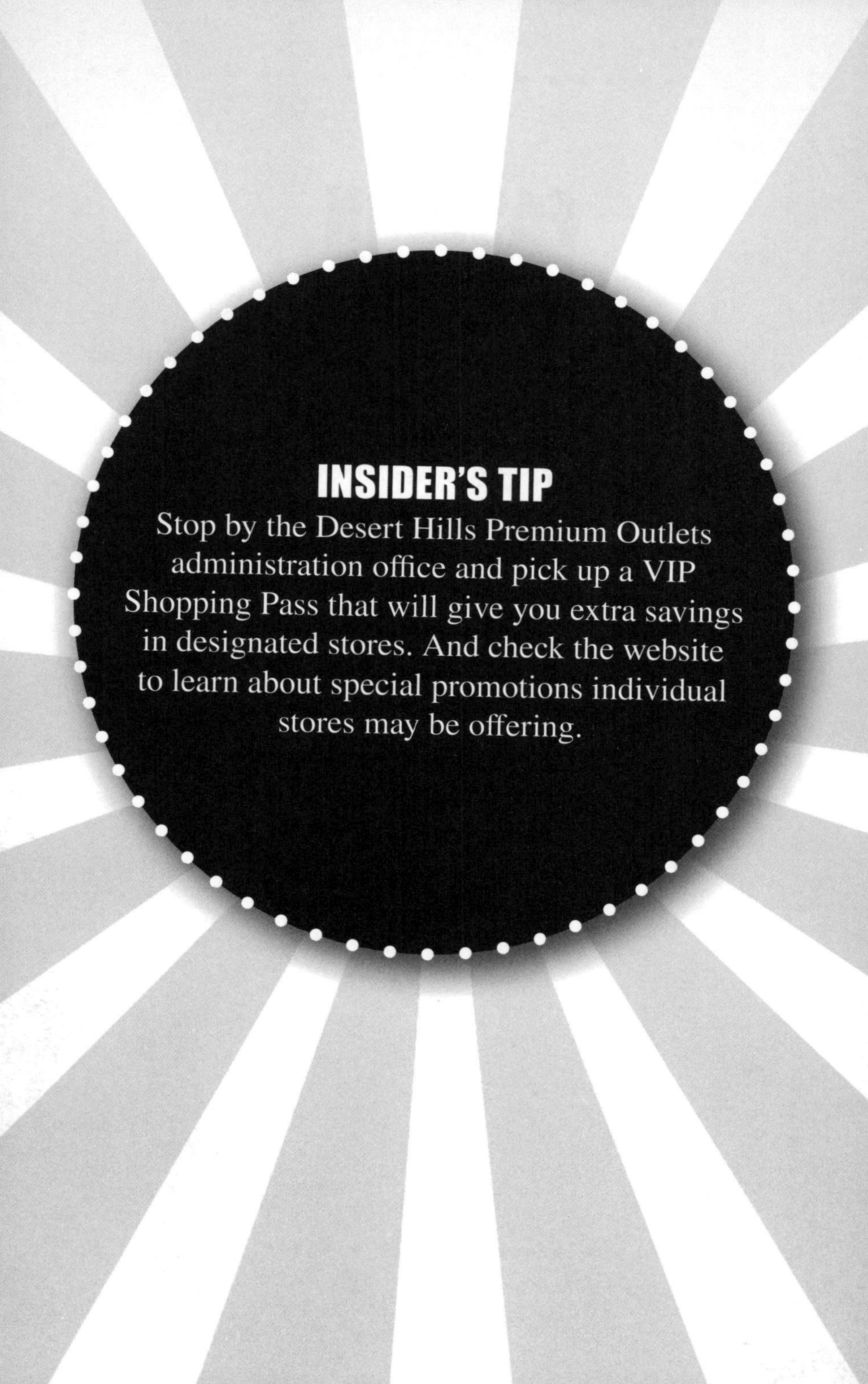
INSIDER'S TIP
Stop by the Desert Hills Premium Outlets administration office and pick up a VIP Shopping Pass that will give you extra savings in designated stores. And check the website to learn about special promotions individual stores may be offering.

96

FASHION
REDUX

For bargain hunters, consignment shopping is about the most fun you can have. And the Coachella Valley is famous for its numerous superb consignments retailers, which you'll find in every city. Whether it's clothing, furniture, or housewares you're looking for, you'll be bound to discover a treasure trove of great finds. But if you're on the hunt for vintage and/or resale designer fashions, you're in luck. During the past few years, the Coachella Valley has become renowned among savvy fashionistas and TV and film producers for the place to score killer resale vintage clothing and designer fashions. Here are just some to check out—happy hunting!

The Frippery/Deja Vu Vintage Finery
664 N. Palm Canyon Drive, Palm Springs
760-699-5365
thefrippery.com

Revivals Resale Mart
611 S. Palm Canyon Drive, Palm Springs
760-318-6430
Several other locations are listed on the website.
revivalsstores.com

Marga's Repeat Boutique
73900 El Paseo, #3 Rear, Palm Desert
760-773-1988
margasrepeatboutique.com

Shirley's Resale Closet
72171 Highway 111, Suite 200, Palm Desert
768-773-4800
shirleysresalecloset.com

ARTFUL
SHOPPING

One of the best-kept secrets about museums is their museum gift shops. They often have really unusual and fabulous finds. The Palm Springs Art Museum Store is no exception. The Museum Store has a selection of one-of-a-kind custom jewelry, creative and educational toys, stylish home décor, art books, and fun gift ideas you won't see elsewhere. The store also hosts occasional trunk shows that showcase the work of national and international studio artists and give the public the rare opportunity to purchase their handcrafted, one-of-a-kind designs. Likewise, the PSAM's other facility, the Architecture & Design Center's Bradford W. Bates Vault: The Museum Design Store (so named because it's housed in a former bank vault), sells architecture and design books and unique jewelry and gift items that showcase exceptional contemporary design.

The Museum Store
Palm Springs Art Museum, 101 Museum Drive, Palm Springs
760-322-4800
psmuseum.org/museum-store

The Vault: The Museum Design Store
Architecture & Design Center, 300 S. Palm Canyon Drive, Palm Springs
760-423-5264
psmuseum.org/architecture-design-center/store

98

SHOP NEW
IN OLD TOWN

Make your way to Old Town La Quinta and step back in time to Old California. Old Town La Quinta is a charming and walkable square with the Spanish architecture of a quaint early California village. Stroll the meandering village streets populated with dozens of boutiques, bistros, and coffee shops. Shop at some of the signature boutiques. Dine alfresco at Stuft Pizza & Grill, Solano's Bistro, or The Grill on Main. Sip wine at La Rue Café Wine Bar or a brew in La Quinta Brewery's Old Town Taproom. Listen to live entertainment in the square. Some of the shopping options are Elizabeth and Prince, Le Chateau Boutique, and As Time Goes By Boutique. Or pick up a gift for a special someone at Gracie's Emporium or Legacy Jewelry.

Old Town La Quinta
78100 Main Street, La Quinta
760-777-1770
oldtownlaquinta.com

99

THE DESIGN "HOOD"

It may come as a surprise when you arrive at the Perez Art and Design Center that you are in a dynamic enclave of some of the best vintage shopping in Southern California. Located in an unassuming strip mall of a Cathedral City industrial neighborhood, this spot has been discovered by L.A. and New York designers and has even caught the attention of *Vogue* magazine. Located on Perez Road in a nondescript business district, the design hub comprises several notable shops specializing in midcentury modern décor—the undisputable brand of Palm Springs. Among these über-cool shops are: Hedge, which has a following of discriminating collectors from all over Southern California; JP Denmark which, as the name implies, offers vintage Danish modern; and @Hom, which has a variety of new and vintage furnishings and accessories.

Hedge
68929 Perez Road #F,
Cathedral City
760-770-0090
hedgepalmsprings.com

JP Denmark
68733 Perez Road, #C-14,
Cathedral City
760-408-9147
jpantik.com

@Hom
68929 Perez Road, Cathedral City
760-770-4447
at-hom.com

TAKE ME
TO THE RIVER

The River in Rancho Mirage brings together the synergy of an exciting shopping, dining, and entertainment destination. The center's unusual design is a big part of the fun, with a large body of water that snakes around the buildings, creating an inviting water oasis. Shopping options abound here—Forever 21, Raymond | Lawrence, Diane's Beachwear, and MAC are just a few. You can also catch a film at a multiscreen movie theater, listen to a musical performance in The River's amphitheater, treat yourself to an ice cream cone at Ben & Jerry's, relax with a cappuccino on the plaza, or dine at one of several eateries, including The Cheesecake Factory, P.F. Chang's, Flemings Steakhouse, or The Yardhouse, among others.

The River
71800 Highway 111, Rancho Mirage
760-341-2711
theriveratranchomirage.com

SUGGESTED ITINERARIES

EXPLORE OUTDOORS

FAMILY-FRIENDLY FUN

ARCHITECTURAL HERITAGE

Palm Springs Modern Tours, 106
O'Donnell House, 114
McCallum Adobe, 115
The Modern Tour, 106
Cornelia White House, 115
ModSquad Architecture & Design Tours, 106
Modernism Week, 113

HISTORY DISCOVERY

Coachella Valley History Museum, 110
Agua Caliente Cultural Museum, 94
Palm Springs Historical Society, 115
Cabot's Pueblo Museum, 95
Palm Springs Air Museum, 112
La Quinta Museum, 111

THE SOUND OF MUSIC

Opera in the Park, 49
Coachella Valley Music and Arts Festival, 42
Palm Springs Women's Jazz Festival, 43
Frank DiSalvo Show, 52
Stagecoach Country Music Festival, 43

ART SMART

Palm Springs Art Museum, 96
Backstreet Art District, 98
La Quinta Arts Festival, 103
Palm Springs Fine Art Fair, 104
The Galen, Palm Springs Art Museum, Palm Desert, 96

TASTY TREATS

Shields Date Garden, 25

Brandini Toffee, 27

Palm Springs Fudge & Chocolates, 27

Desert Tasty Tours, 26

CATCH THE VIEWS

Palms to Pines Scenic Byway, 58

Fantasy Balloons, 80

Palm Springs Biplanes, 83

Salton Sea State Recreational Area, 58

Lookout Lounge—PS Aerial Tramway, 20

HIGH DESERT ADVENTURE

Joshua Tree National Park, 66

Pioneertown, 88

Pappy & Harriet's Pioneertown Palace, 88

Integratron, 68

Mojave Trails National Monument, 72

RETRO AND VINTAGE SHOPPING

DIVINE DESIGN

LOVE TO SHOP

INDEX